# More Than a Ballgame ...
## An Inside Look at Minor League Baseball

by **Sam Lazzaro**

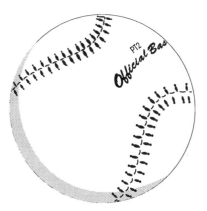

Published by
**Pocahontas Press, Inc.**
Blacksburg, Virginia

More Than a Ballgame ...
An Inside Look at Minor League Baseball
by **Sam Lazzaro**

**Cover design** by **Lezlie Williams,** Laughing Crow Studio, Mission, South Dakota

Published by Pocahontas Press, Inc., Blacksburg, Virginia, U.S.A.

Printed in the United States of America by Christiansburg Printing, Christiansburg, Virginia.

First printing, 1997
ISBN 0-936015-71-3

Library of Congress Cataloging-in-Publication Data:

    Lazzaro, Sam. 1944 –
      More than a ballgame: An inside look at minor league baseball / by Sam Lazzaro.
      p.     cm.
      Includes index.
      ISBN 0-936015-71-3
      1. Minor league baseball--United States. 2. Lazzaro, Sam.
    I. Title.
    GV863.A1L29    1997
    796.357'64--dc21

                                      97-18355
                                          CIP

# Dedication

This book is dedicated to the memory of two great baseball fans who had an impact on my life: my grandfather, Gerald Dunn, a true-blue Brooklyn Dodgers fan, who instilled in me my love of the game. Noonie, my time with you was too short.

And Bennie Cernaro, an avid Yankee fan, who lost his will to live during the strike of '94. As a youngster, I spent hours talking baseball with him. It is with these fond memories of green infield grass and simpler times that this book was written.

# Contents

# Foreword

It had been a remarkable decade and a half for minor league baseball. In 1983 when Sam Lazarro entered minor league baseball in Elmira, New York, the minors were still the bush leagues. Minor league franchises had little value, attendance was spotty, and most ball parks were old and decrepit.

For a brief period after World War II, minor league baseball boomed. In 1949 with 438 teams in 59 leagues, every town, city, and village that considered itself anything boasted of a professional team. But the minor leagues could not maintain that success, and for the next thirty years the minors endured a long downhill slide. Some blamed television, others air conditioning, and for many it was simply the changing tastes of the American people. For all these reasons and more, the minors plummeted, and by the 1970s there were barely 100 teams in some 15 leagues. Minor league baseball was kept alive by the major leagues because the big leagues felt the only way to develop talent was through a minor league system.

In the late 1970s and early 1980s there were indications that things might change. Sporadic successes erupted in such cities as Columbus, and Nashville, and El Paso. The Viet Nam nightmare was over, and Americans wanted to return to more traditional pastimes. The rise in major league prices made minor league baseball an affordable alternative, and the development of sports administration programs started preparing young people for entry into the business end of the sport.

Everything began looking up, and the trickle of successful teams became a stream, and then a torrent.

Sam Lazarro has seen the changes. He has been part of the game during this remarkable period of growth, and he has become one of the most respected operators in the game. Sam dealt with the con men and the quick buck artists who populated the game in the years when he was starting. He has had to dodge bill collectors, has seen paychecks bounce, and has wondered why he was still in the game. But it is good people like Sam Lazarro who have helped bring the game to the status it enjoys today. Now, with multimillion dollar stadiums, sellouts, and national recognition, the sport that was once on life support has changed dramatically.

*More Than a Ball Game: An Inside Look at Minor League Baseball* is a great picture of the changes the sport has seen. Moreover, it is a picture of the hard work, long hours, and difficulties it has taken to run a successful minor league franchise. Sam Lazzaro has pulled the tarps, sold the fence signs, cleaned the bathrooms, and cooked the hot dogs. He has seen the future major leaguers and the players on their way out. For those who have been in the game, he tells the truth; those who haven't will experience what it's like to run a minor league franchise. The rise of minor league baseball is a tremendous success story in modern America. Sam Lazzaro tells it well.

Miles Wolff

July 1997

# Preface

The purpose of this book is to present an inside look at the game of baseball. It is not an attempt to show the game from a player's perspective but, instead, through the eyes of someone who has worked in the professional game for a number of years.

You'll read about players like Moises Alou, Ellis Burks, Brady Anderson, Wes Chamberlain, Mitch Williams, Lenny Dykstra, Gregg Jefferies, and Dwight Gooden. Sparky Lyle, Dave Parker, and legendary manager Rocky Bridges all come to life in this true account of some of baseball's minor league teams.

You'll meet a club owner who made a habit of firing five employees each week to keep his sales staff on its toes (and it wasn't George Steinbrenner). You'll meet another who operated the worst franchise in baseball.

I've tried to capture the atmosphere of all facets of minor league life, through my own personal experiences. My career has been an emotional roller coaster ride — from the players and coaches, to the multi-faceted promotional events, the wins and losses, weather and field problems, some humor, some sadness, many personalities, and many characters.

This book presents a different side of our great national pastime. Many of the events described herein prove the old adage that truth is indeed stranger than fiction.

The Salem Buccaneers, 1987 Carolina League champions. From left, front row: Gilberto Roca, Mike Dotzler, Bill Copp, Reggie Barringer, Steve Moser, Mike Stevanus, Tim Kirk, Matias Carrillo. Middle row: Manager Steve Demeter, Mike Walker, Doug Pittman, Greg Stading, Larry Melton, Bob Koopmann, Bill Sampen, Rob Hatfield, Jeff King, Kevin Davis. Back row: Vice-President of Baseball Operations Sam Lazzaro, Trainer Harold Williams, Martin Hernandez, Ben Morrow, Jose Melendez, Pete Rice, Tony Chance, Scott Little, John Rigos, Todd Smith, Pitching Coach Chris Lein, Director of Broadcasting Brian Barnhart, General Manager Jon Kaufman.

The 1988 Salem Buccaneers. From left, front row: Kevin Burdick, Chip Duncan, Ben Webb, Andy Hall, Ed Yacopino, John Love, Julio Peguero, Oscar Escobar, Tony Longmire, Junior Vizcaino. Middle row: Doug Torborg, Clyde Reichard, Scott Henion, Terry Crowley, Tim McKinley, Tom Shields, Rick Reed, Stan Belinda, Tim Kirk. Back row: Mike York, Scott Ruskin, Pete Murphy, Steve Adams, Administrative Assistant Torree Selders, Vice-president/General Manager Sam Lazzaro, Manager Jay Ward, Assistant General Manager Jim Tessmer, Stadium Supervisor Sam Clark, Keith Raisanen, Pitching Coach Chris Lein, Trainer Bruce Klein.

# Acknowledgments

I'd like to express my appreciation to the many
people who helped make this book a reality. Among
them, Bobby Bragan Jr. for giving me my first opportunity to run a ballclub; Kelvin Bowles, for convincing
me that Salem was the right place to further my baseball
education; Jack Bogaczyk, a real writer, who steered me
in the right direction with constructive criticism and
sound advice; The Valley Writers Club, for giving me
the confidence to push forward in my quest to find a
publisher; Mary Holliman and Pocahontas Press for
becoming that publisher, taking a chance on an unpub-
lished author; David Bruce Wallace and Diana
Kittleman of Pocahontas Press for their time and effort
in putting the book together; Miles Wolff and *Baseball
America*, for providing tremendous sources of baseball
information; Brian Hoffman and Dan Keel, who served
as team photographers in Salem and Elmira respectively
and provided many of the pictures found in this book; to
all of the fans and sponsors that helped make the clubs I
worked with successful over the years; to all of my staff
personnel and co-workers for doing a great job and
making me look good; and especially to my wife Sue,
for making many sacrifices while I wrote this book,
serving as a sounding board, and always being beside
me in baseball and in life, despite all I've put her
through.

# The Sam Lazzaro Time Line

1983 — Sam Lazzaro's first job in baseball with Elmira Suns, short-season A affiliate of the Boston Red Sox in New York-Penn League.

1984 — Bobby Bragan takes ownership in Elmira. Team nickname changed to Pioneers. SL named NY-P League Executive of the Year.

1985 — SL receives NY-P MacPhail Award for promotional excellence.

1986 — SL joins Salem Redbirds, Advanced A affiliate of Texas Rangers in Carolina League.

1987 — Salem Buccaneers win Carolina League championship in first year of Pittsburgh Pirates affiliation.

1988 — Buccaneers again make Carolina League playoffs.

1989 — Too much rain. SL named Carolina League Executive of the Year.

1990 — Pittsburgh Pirates win first of three consecutive NL East titles. New Professional Baseball Agreement enacted following threat to do away with minor leagues.

1991 — We are ripped off by a concert promoter. Pirates continue winning ways, but again fail to reach World Series.

1992 — Hosting Carolina League All-Star Game. Celebrating 25 years in Carolina League. Former Buc Tim Wakefield shines. Pirates lose in NLCS on dramatic 9th inning rally by Braves in seventh game.

1993 — Major League baseball dumps commissioner.
Marge Shott in trouble again.
1994 — Salem club sold, then unsold; new stadium approved.
Michael Jordan retires from NBA to play pro baseball.
Major leaguers go on strike; no World Series.
1995 — Salem team affiliated with Colorado Rockies, becomes
Salem Avalanche. Michael Jordan returns to NBA.
Salem Memorial Baseball Stadium opens on August
7th. Major leaguers return; Cal Ripken breaks consecutive games record.
1996 — New stadium finally completed. SL leaves Salem club.

## Photo Credits:

I thank the following persons for permitting me to use their
photographs in this book.

Brian Hoffman and *The Salem Times Register*:
  pages 22, 57, 62, 63, 67, 79, 94, 103, 109, 113, 119, 121,
  125, 129, 135, 139, 141, 143, 145, 151, 164, 167, 169, 175,
  179, 189, 191, 193, 215, 239, 241, 245, 251, 253, 259.

Dan Keel Photography:
  pages 13, 15, 16, 19, 31, 39, 40, 45.

Gentry Studios: pages viii, ix, 209.

Barbara Peterson: page 201.

National Association of Professional Baseball Leagues:
  page 132.

# How Did I Get Into This Mess Anyway?

Climbing the concrete grandstand to the office in a blustery January wind while trying to avoid slipping on the hard-packed snow and ice wasn't quite what I'd envisioned baseball life to be. But that was how I began my baseball career.

It all started innocently enough right after the Christmas holidays. It was January 1983 when I spotted a blind box ad in *The Sporting News*, looking for individuals interested in careers as professional baseball executives. Sales experience was required, sports experience was not. I had both.

I had graduated from the State University of New York at Oswego in 1977, with a B.A. in communication studies. I had decided to become a sports reporter after I'd given up my dream to play pro baseball when I realized that my desire far outweighed my ability. I took several journalism courses in college and, after getting over my initial shyness, found myself attracted to the broadcasting side of the business.

I worked as a sports broadcaster at the college radio and television stations while a student, and, during my final two years of school, was the play-by-play announcer for hockey. After graduation, my hockey experience got me my first commercial radio job when I was hired by my hometown radio station WSGO, to handle the play-by-play duties for high school football games.

Unfortunately, at a small hometown radio station, the position of high school play-by-play announcer is rarely a full-time job. This station was no exception. To work full-time, I had to handle other duties.

I auditioned for an opening as the afternoon disc jockey but lost out to Jay Schadler, another recent college grad who had applied for the job after graduating from law school at Syracuse University. We eventually became close friends. Jay later moved on to bigger and better things, serving as a network correspondent for ABC News, then becoming a correspondent for the "Prime Time Live" and "Day One" news magazine shows, and hosting The Justice Files" on the Discovery Channel.

After a brief stint as a disc jockey at another radio station, I received a call from the owner of WSGO who told me he had an opening for a salesperson. After discussing the position with him, I decided to give it a try. Though I had no real sales experience, he was willing to give me an opportunity. Learning about sales was one of the best decisions I made, as it has opened many doors for me.

I spent a little over two years at WSGO as a full-time salesperson and a part-time sportscaster, before I was ready to make my big move. I was hired as the director of marketing and public relations for a minor league professional ice hockey team, the Utica Mohawks. The team was in the process of moving from Utica, New York to Salem, Virginia, and their director of marketing & public relations was not interested in making the 600-mile journey. So with my wife and seven-month-old son, I headed south in late July, looking to make a name and career in pro hockey.

As it turned out, I gained valuable experience. For one thing, I learned to look before leaping. Selling hockey in the south was not the easiest thing I ever did. To add to the difficulty, the first thing we did every morning upon arriving at the office was to check the telex machine to be sure the league was still operating. Not much security for a young family. Being our first time really away from all of our friends and relatives, we were homesick as well.

As the doldrums of the season progressed, and the money got tighter and tighter, it was plain to see this was not exactly what I had in mind when leaving the comfort of radio. I resigned and we returned north in March to seek a little more stability.

I went back to work in radio in Syracuse, New York, handling nothing but sales for WOLF, one of the better known Syracuse stations. WOLF claimed the distinction of having started the careers of both Dick Clark and Marv Albert, who had worked there while students at Syracuse University. WOLF was in the process of being sold and was changing from its popular rock 'n roll to an automated country format.

The most important thing I gained from my employment at WOLF was an extensive and on-going training in sales. Since I already had some sales experience, this highly specialized training was exactly what was needed to prepare me for a career requiring strong skills in sales, marketing, and promotion.

After six months at WOLF, I was offered a much better position at a competing station, WSEN. The station manager at WSEN began to take notice when I grabbed a number of their accounts and brought them to WOLF. He called and made me an offer I couldn't refuse.

Despite my now successful sales career in radio, boredom was beginning to set in. I missed the excitement of the sports world, but had vowed when I left hockey not to take a job in sports again unless there was a great deal of security in the position. I was convinced that I had probably experienced my one and only job in pro sports. But I looked at that ad in *The Sporting News* and thought about it. A career as an executive in baseball. I could live with that. But could my wife and now three-year-old son?

The more I looked at that ad, the more I tried to convince myself that the job wasn't for me. I finally succeeded and forgot about it, until the following week when my new issue of *The Sporting News* arrived and I saw the ad again. I finally said, "What the heck?" and sent off a copy of my resume without even including a cover letter. I felt certain I was wasting my time and would never hear from the party at the other end of the blind box.

I was totally shocked when I received a letter from a company called Baseball Enterprises, Inc., a week or so later informing me they were impressed with my resume and would like to schedule an appointment to talk with me. The letter was signed by Bobby Bragan Jr., a name that certainly rang a bell with me since I'd been following pro baseball for so many years.

I showed the letter to Sue, my wife, who said, "I had a feeling something was going to happen when you sent off your resume. It's something you have to do. If you don't, you'll regret it for the rest of your life."

I called the phone number given on the letter and spoke with Bobby Bragan Jr. for the first time. I learned that he was vice president of the company, which owned five minor league baseball teams — in Jacksonville, Florida; Peoria, Illinois; Florence, South Carolina; Hagerstown, Maryland; and Elmira, New York. They were looking at possibly expanding their operations by purchasing a team in each of the sixteen minor leagues that were in operation.

Only a handful of minor league clubs are owned by their major league affiliates. The majority are owned and operated by individuals, groups, or corporations as independent businesses affiliated with the major league clubs. All of the players,

*Is this really where it all began? Doubleday Field, Cooperstown, New York*

coaches, and managers are employed by the major league club and assigned to the affiliate. The franchise operator is primarily responsible for running the business side of the club. Both parties have certain obligations that are clearly spelled out in a binding document, the "Player Development Contract" (PDC).

Bobby was planning to fly into Syracuse the following week to check on the Elmira team. His organization had just made a change in GMs and he was planning to add additional staff. I had some vacation time coming at the radio station and decided to take advantage of this opportunity. I offered to pick Bobby up at the airport in Syracuse and drive him to Elmira. Later, when I talked with Bobby again to finalize details, he told me that Lou Eliopulos, president and owner of Baseball Enterprises, would also be joining us.

During the two-hour drive from Syracuse to Elmira we talked extensively about their plans to build a baseball empire. I was impressed that I might have the opportunity to work in pro baseball, especially for an organization that appeared to be growing tremendously. By the time we reached our destination, the so-called "beautiful Dunn Field," it was late in the afternoon and Dunn Field really didn't look so beautiful covered with a cold, crusty January snow.

The office was at the top of the concrete grandstand. The cold January windchill we encountered while walking up the concourse steps to the office wasn't very baseball-like, either. In the office I met the longtime secretary of the team, Jean Hoffman, a woman in her early sixties who had spent many years working for the Elmira club under a number of owners and operators.

I also met Dick Radatz Jr., a recent graduate of the sports administration Masters program at Ohio University. Dick is the son of the famous Red Sox relief pitcher of the '60s, Dick "The Monster" Radatz. Dick Jr. had been hired by Baseball Enterprises at the Baseball Winter Meetings in December. When the opening for a GM with their Elmira team occurred, Radatz was a good choice, with Elmira being a Red Sox farm club.

After a short while at the office, I was instructed to return early the next day ready to hit the streets and make some sales. I left the office excited about getting a chance to work in baseball.

My excitement quickly disappeared the following morning when I arrived for work. There were cars all over the parking lot and people everywhere as I climbed the stadium steps to the office. I could have understood if this had been a game day, but it was late January and there was snow on the ground. As I walked into the office, I realized that all of these people also were looking for jobs in baseball. Lou had run an ad in the local newspaper and it appeared the entire city had responded.

As I was about to learn, this was the way Lou operated. Every person that showed up with a serious interest in working was hired immediately and given a brochure showing the prices of outfield fence signs, souvenir program ads, and season ticket packages. We were then handed several contracts with instructions to go make sales and pushed out the door. So much for feeling special about working in baseball!

I hit the streets, and fortunately made a couple of quick program ad sales. I also found myself running into a number of fellow salespeople all over town. Many of the businesses I visited had already been solicited by several from the swarm of salespeople who hit the streets that morning.

This was how Lou liked to blanket a town. This, despite the fact that local merchants were getting upset because there were more salespeople from the Elmira Suns than customers in their stores. Of course, that wasn't totally surprising, considering that in January 1983 Elmira had the highest unemployment rate in New York State — about 24 percent.

I returned to the office late in the afternoon with several signed contracts and several more good leads that looked promising over the next few days. A number of people were leaving dejectedly. As I was to find out, those who returned without a signed contract were told their services were no longer needed. Those bringing in a contract would live to see at least one more day as a baseball executive.

That's right! That's the way Lou ran his ballclubs.

Now that I knew the rules of the game, I thought that maybe this wasn't worth giving up my secure radio position for, after all. But I also knew I could sell and I was willing to at least finish the week to see how things worked out. Being on vacation, all I had to lose at this point was my time off.

I'd been making good progress with Robinson Lumber on an outfield billboard package, and had already signed many new advertisers including Midas Muffler, Overhead Door Company, and Lums Restaurant. Both Midas and Lums had purchased lucky number program ads, meaning they would provide prizes to be given away during every game in exchange for public address announcements drawing attention to their ads. During these public address announcements a "lucky number" is announced, and the holder of the program with the correct number wins that prize. I was also using my radio connections to line up meetings with several Syracuse based companies with locations in Elmira, including Fay's Drug Stores, P&C Food Markets, and Eastern Copy Products.

I continued to sign advertising contracts all week and, as expected, the crew meeting in the office was shrinking each day. By the end of the week, I was one of only three people along with Radatz, remaining. A decision had to be made. Bobby Bragan offered me the assistant GM's job. I kept reminding myself about the vow I had made not to accept a position with no security, but deep down inside I knew this was what I wanted to do.

I accepted the job despite a salary offer of only $800 per month. The money was considerably less than I was making, but I just had to follow my dream. Bobby also promised to set up a commission structure and an override benefit on sales to help supplement my salary. If I had known then that Lou would overrule him on both counts, I probably would not have accepted the offer. It was several months before I became aware of Lou's decision, and by then it was too late. I already was committed.

I do have one thing for which to thank Lou. I certainly learned how to sell under pressure. He was based in Jacksonville, Fla., working out of the office of his Jacksonville Suns.

Every afternoon either Lou's secretary Carolyn, Bobby Bragan, or Lou would call to see what we had sold that day. Our front office staff had dwindled to myself, Radatz, and Jean Hoffman. With Dick and me handling all sales, we were able to keep enough contracts coming in to keep Lou off our backs. Unfortunately, not everyone in the organization could say the same thing.

Lou liked competition among his salespeople. Because Elmira was a short-season club in the New York-Penn League, we had the smallest sales staff in his organization. His other four clubs had anywhere from five to 10 salespeople each. Every couple of weeks Lou would set up a new contest based on weekly sales and money collected. Each salesperson in the organization would accumulate points based on total sales and collections. Every Friday afternoon, Carolyn would call each club to get the sales information. We would sit in the office waiting for the telex machine to begin operating. After all sales figures were tabulated, each club would receive the contest "standings". The top five salespeople in the organization received top billing and some complimentary remarks after their names on the telex message. The people in the middle would receive some chiding or derogatory remarks imploring them to pick up the pace. The bottom five finishers every week had "retired" next to their names. They were terminated. I realized I must avoid the bottom five positions if I wanted to continue working in baseball.

To most people Lou came across as a cold-hearted operator. He rubbed many people the wrong way and gave minor league baseball a bad name at a time it was just beginning to take off. Lou was a difficult man to get to know, but eventually I did get to see another side of him.

Deep inside, Lou was very generous, so much so that it eventually led to his baseball downfall. At one time nearly every member of his large family, including in-laws, was on his payroll. Unfortunately, only a few were contributing any work.

Lou attempted to build a minor league empire by putting an emphasis on sales at a time when very few clubs were sales oriented. He had some good ideas and hired a number of very good people. If he had been able to hang on just a few more years, he probably would have retired a very rich man, based on the value of minor league franchises today.

It was my understanding that Lou had very little of his own money invested in the corporation. He financed or carried notes on all of the clubs and needed a tremendous cash flow each month to make his payments. It was just another reason he demanded such a strong emphasis on sales from his people.

Lou drove a new Cadillac and Bobby a Lincoln Continental. Both drew big salaries, and had large expense accounts. Those were just some of the things that eventually led to the downfall of the expansion plans and ultimately forced Lou to sell or give away all of his clubs.

As a result, it was rare for anyone in the organization besides Lou, Bobby, or Lou's family members to receive a paycheck on time. And thus, after we had waited sometimes as long as two weeks past payday to receive our paychecks, the check often bounced. It became a routine to call the bank each time we received our paychecks, to be sure funds were available. Often, there weren't.

Because we made the deposits when money came in from Elmira advertisers and ticket holders, we eventually figured out that we could hold back on depositing some of the money until our paychecks arrived.We would then simultaneously deposit the advertising money and cash our paychecks. This method wasn't foolproof because the account was sometimes overdrawn by more than our advertising revenue could balance, but for the most part it did improve our chances of getting paid.

# 2  What An Act To Follow!

That winter of 1983 was memorable. Before I accepted the job in Elmira, no one knew much about why Lou and Bobby were making changes in the front office. It didn't take long to find out.

Apparently there was a discrepancy regarding money players from the '82 team had given to the previous General Manager, Thom Shannon, to cover their rent in an agreement the ballclub had with Elmira College. To provide quality housing for their players, the parent Red Sox, in conjunction with the Elmira club, worked out an arrangement whereby the players lived in campus dormitories each summer. This worked out extremely well for both parties. With the New York-Penn a short season league, players arrived in town in early June, starting their season after the majority of college students had gone home for the summer.

Thus the college generated additional revenue by renting dorm space to the players at a time the rooms normally would have been vacant. The only problem was the college had never received all of the money owed by the 1982 team. The money had supposedly been collected by Shannon, who was to pay the college. For some reason, payment was never made.

As a result, Lou and Bobby were involved in an ongoing investigation of Shannon, had already fired him, and were in the process of filing criminal charges against him. Additionally, they were trying to keep this information confidential to avoid the very negative publicity that would be linked to the club.

So here we were, in a city with an unemployment rate of 24 percent, trying to sell professional baseball, knowing full well that what was a difficult job could become nearly impossible if the wrong people learned this information.

To make matters worse, the GM preceding Shannon, Marve Handler, also had a reputation of not always being on the up and up. As we would make our sales calls in the community, quite often his name would be brought into the conversation, along with some supposedly diabolical deed he had done. In fact, credibility was something for which very few of the previous club operators were noted.

Handler had also owned part of the club before selling out to Lou, primarily for the debt the club owed. That was a common practice in minor league baseball at that time, prior to the rapid escalation of franchise values. Handler had remained in town, working as a sportscaster for one of the local television stations. Later, while still working at the television station, he was indicted for stealing checks from mailboxes in his apartment building. Stolen merchandise was also found in his car and apartment during the subsequent investigation.

Needless to say, we were not always welcomed with open arms when we went out on sales calls. Nevertheless, we continued to plug away, making as many sales as possible and lining up a fairly extensive promotional schedule for the upcoming season. With Elmira's high unemployment rate, the downtown area was reminiscent of a ghost town. A number of storefronts were boarded up. We concentrated on regional businesses with out-of-town headquarters and, with my radio contacts in the nearby Syracuse market, we were able to bring in much needed new business.

Finally, June arrived and with it came our manager and ballplayers. The season opened, and Dunn Field finally was alive with the sounds of summer and baseball. Having survived

*Elmira's beautiful Dunn Field.*

the long, cold and eventful winter, we were excited about getting started.

Dunn Field always has been one of the finest ballparks in the country for a short season or a rookie league. It was built in 1938, following a fire that burned down the original structure. Unfortunately, because of its location, on the banks of the Chemung River, it had to be closed for five weeks during the 1946 season due to flooding. The waters of the Chemung took an even greater toll on Dunn Field in 1972, when the ballpark was almost destroyed and the bulk of the entire season was wiped out by a major flood brought on by hurricane Agnes.

In 1975, Dunn Field was beginning to show signs of age and some major repairs were done. But by 1978 the ballpark was in need of still more extensive repairs and a decision had to be made. The "Save Dunn Field Committee" was formed, with the task of raising funds for the old ballpark. The effort was successful, leading to the passing of a bond issue in April 1978 that gave the ballpark new life.

As a result of its efforts, the "Dunn Field Committee" had a great deal of control over the use of the facility. In conjunction with the city, the group provided maintenance for the field, including handling the groundskeeping in the evenings during our ballgames. The city provided a groundskeeper during weekdays, but in the evenings and on weekends the field was handled by volunteers representing the "Dunn Field Committee." During bad weather conditions, this arrangement seldom worked to our advantage. We found it difficult to motivate an all-volunteer crew when the going got tough, as it did during rains.

A major reason Dunn Field is one of the finest short season or rookie league facilities is that it was originally built as a home to teams in more advanced leagues. In fact, before the New York-Penn League moved into Dunn Field in 1973, the park was the home of franchises in the Class Double-A Eastern League. From 1962-68, the Baltimore Orioles Double-A club won two pennants and never finished out of the first division. Earl Weaver managed the 1964 pennant winner, while the 1966 Elmira club won the Eastern League pennant by a record 22 1/2 games behind manager Darrell Johnson.

Baltimore pulled out of Elmira after the '68 season and in 1969 San Diego and Kansas City shared the working agreement. In 1970 Kansas City took over the full agreement but decided to pull out after the 1971 season, selling the franchise to Kip Horsburgh and Carl Fazio. They set up a working agreement with the Cleveland Indians for the 1972 season, but the flood of '72 ruined the ballpark and the owners lost a bundle of money. They then sold the franchise to a group that moved the team to Waterbury, Connecticut.

*Pro Baseball's youngest batboy Sammy Lazzaro, at age 3, racing to the dugout with a bat at Elmira's Dunn Field, in 1983.*

This move led to the entrance of the New York-Penn League at Elmira when Joe Romano, owner of the Williamsport club, decided to move his team into vacant Dunn Field. Several owners followed Romano, with Eliopulos taking ownership in 1982.

The 1983 season was a lot of fun. Despite a slow start, we had a talented group of players, and they improved as the season progressed. We ended the season with a five-game winning streak to pull above .500 for the only time all year. We placed three players on the final New York-Penn League All-Star Team despite finishing the season with a record just two games over .500 (38-36).Our shortstop, Rey Quinones, outfielder Paul Thoutsis, and pitcher Hector Stewart were named all-stars. We also had a center fielder named Ellis Burks and a pitcher named Dana Kiecker.

*Elmira Suns in 1983: (from left) Jesus Silva, Pat Jelks, Sammy Lazzaro, Ellis Burks, Rich Winfield, Jose Birrel.*

Our manager was Dick Berardino, a disciplinarian, known for doing a great job with the young Red Sox players. Dick spent many years managing the Red Sox' first step up the ladder before finally being promoted in the organization. He eventually served as a coach with the major league team.

Shortstop Quinones was named as one of the players in the league most likely to succeed. He eventually played for Boston in 1986 before being traded to Seattle in August for Spike Owen and Dave Henderson. After several seasons with the Mariners he was traded to Pittsburgh in 1989 and eventually released. Burks probably has been the most successful player to come from that 1983 Elmira team. He was just a skinny 18-year-old with very good speed but not much power. He hit only .241 that year, but the Red Sox liked his potential and continued to work with him. He eventually made it to "The Show" with Boston in 1987 and hit twenty home runs his rookie season. He's become an excellent major leaguer, hitting .344 with 40 HR's, 128 RBI and 32 stolen bases for Colorado in 1996.

We also had a young pitcher named John Mitchell. He turned 18 late in the '83 season. He started off slowly but then came on strong. He was traded to the Mets organization after the 1985 season and in '86 was named the Pitcher of the Year in the Triple-A International League before being called up to the New York Mets. He spent parts of the next three seasons with the Mets before being traded to Baltimore, where he finished his big league career in 1990 with a record of 6-6.

In addition, we had an even younger pitcher — 15-year-old Josias Manzanillo, from that incredible baseball city of San Pedro de Macoris in the Dominican Republic. Manzanillo went just 1-5, but despite his youth showed potential with a live fastball. He ended up pitching parts of the 1984 and 1985 seasons in Elmira as well, before finally moving up the ladder.

Unlike many of the clubs in the New York-Penn League, the Red Sox used Elmira as their Rookie League team. Most other parent clubs used the NY-P League as a step up from their rookie league teams, meaning many of Elmira's opponents were a bit more experienced. By the end of the season, our club was able to hold its own with any team in our league, including the veteran Utica Blue Sox.

Utica had an older team made up of castoffs and released players from many organizations. The team was owned by a group headed by Miles Wolff and included comedian Bill Murray. They operated as an independent franchise, meaning they had no major league affiliate. Most of their players had played at higher classifications before being cut by their major league clubs. Prior to the start of the season, Roger Kahn was named president of the team and spent the entire season traveling with the club while writing a book called *Good Enough To Dream*. It's an excellent book, accurately depicting the lives of players in the lower minor leagues.

The veteran bunch from Utica eventually won the league championship, but not without some difficulty. Our young club was intimidated and badly outclassed during our early season meetings, but came back to sweep a big doubleheader from the Blue Sox late in the year, enabling the Little Falls Mets to get very close and take the divisional race down to the wire before finally being edged by Utica.

With a crowd of over 3,000 in attendance for a between games pitching demonstration by Hall-Of-Famer Bob Feller on August 19, our pitchers put on a display of their own in silencing the potent Utica bats. Dana Kiecker went the distance in the first game, scattering six hits in winning his fifth in a row, 5-1. Andy Estrada's RBI triple and a run scoring single by Paul Thoutsis provided the margin of victory. The second game saw two of our relievers, Omar Bencomo and Mike Dalton, combine on a four hitter in a 2-1 win, keyed by first baseman Jose Birriel's two-run first inning homer.

One of the biggest events in Elmira baseball history took place at Dunn Field early in the season. We hosted an "Old Timers' Game", with 55 former Elmira players invited to participate and 52 actually showing up for the event, including former manager Earl Weaver, along with Pat Gillick, Eddie Robinson, Sal Maglie, Tommy Holmes, and Zoilo Versalles.

One other memory that stands out was an incident that occurred in late July. We were playing a night game, as was usually the case, and as twilight began descending, a member of the Dunn Field Committee tending the grounds that night turned on the lights. The bank of lights on the pole behind third base did not come on. Fortunately for us, this member of the Dunn Field Committee had worked the field several nights

*Myself, Bob Feller, and Dick Radatz, Jr. in 1983.*

earlier when that same light pole refused to cooperate. He had remedied that situation by banging a big sledgehammer against the pole until, surprisingly, the lights started shining.

We had a major promotion with free tickets provided by a local bank, and the stadium was nearly full. So here, in front of a packed house, we see this man beating on the light pole with a huge sledgehammer. Unfortunately for us, this time it didn't work. The two field managers then went out to discuss the situation with the umpires and decided that without all the lights working, the game would have to be postponed. We had played only a couple of innings so it was not even close to an official game. Reluctantly, we decided we would resume the game at the point of suspension the following evening, then play the regularly scheduled game after that. An electrician fixed the lights the following day, enabling us to proceed with our plans.

We also decided that rather than lose the gate we were anticipating for the following night, we would clear the stands between games, charging the people who had come with rainchecks from the night before for admission to the second game. What a mess! We upset a lot of people, including the sponsor of the promotion from the previous night. Needless to say, we learned from that experience. The extra money generated from charging that second admission didn't come close to compensating for the damage done from a public relations standpoint.

My greatest concern during the season was whether I would keep my job with the ballclub. There was talk that Lou would keep me around only as long as I continued to make sales. Once the season began and the potential to continue bringing in big contracts was over, I was afraid I would be let go. But apparently Lou saw enough in my sales ability to feel that I fit into his long-range plans of expansion.

As the season was winding down, plans were being made for next season. Lou was talking about moving Radatz to another club, and it appeared that club would be located in Spartanburg, South Carolina, in the South Atlantic League. Lou was in the process of selling his Florence team in the same league and as soon as he completed the deal, he planned on buying Spartanburg and sending Radatz in as the new GM. If plans went as expected, I would then be named the new GM in Elmira. At the end of the season an organizational meeting was held in Jacksonville. Both Radatz and I flew in from Elmira and were joined by Dan Overstreet (Lou's GM in Peoria), Bob Miller (the GM in Hagerstown), Mike Ondina, Lou's son-in-law and GM in Jacksonville (who was a first-round draft pick of the White Sox in 1972), and Bobby Bragan Jr. Rory Litz, the GM in Florence, was not included in the meeting because Lou was very close to closing the Florence deal and Rory's future with the organization was up in the air.

The meeting involved two days of discussion among the members of our group, reviewing sales, promotions, marketing, and more. We discussed plans and goals for the 1984 season as well. During the second day, Lou closed the deal on Florence and purchased Spartanburg. He immediately turned to Radatz with the news that he was the new G.M. in Spartanburg. He then informed me that I was the new Elmira GM and we would schedule a news conference shortly after my return to make the official announcement.

Unfortunately for Lou, Radatz had no desire to go to Spartanburg. He had already contacted the Boston Red Sox about the possibility of taking over the Winter Haven GM position. Winter Haven was the full-season Florida State League affiliate of the Red Sox, and Boston also owned the franchise. In addition, Winter Haven housed the Bosox spring training base, making the job an attractive one for Radatz, with the responsibility of setting up spring training for the big league club along with running the Florida State League operation. Unfortunately for Radatz, the Red Sox had not yet decided to offer him the position, so he reluctantly returned with me to Elmira to pack up his belongings and move to Spartanburg.

Shortly after he arrived in Spartanburg, the Red Sox offered Radatz the Winter Haven job, and he accepted. In the meantime, Lou was beginning to run into other problems.

*The famous "San Diego Chicken" trying to distract the visiting pitcher.*

# 3 Grabbing The Reins

On my return to Elmira from the mid-September organizational meeting in Jacksonville, we set up a news conference, and Bobby Bragan flew into town to make the official announcement. I was now in charge of the Elmira franchise and looked forward to the challenge as an opportunity to prove myself.

It didn't take long to begin lining up sales and promotional events for the upcoming season. It felt good to have some time to put things together, unlike during the previous season when we had started working in late January. Everything was going extremely well, and having four extra months to line up events was going to make a big difference.

But all was not going as well for Lou and Baseball Enterprises. Lou's tendency of not paying his bills was beginning to catch up with him. The Midwest League was up in arms over the fact that he had left behind a tremendous amount of debt when he moved his club from Danville to Peoria. Apparently, he also was having money problems in Peoria, and the league was demanding that he sell the club on his terms or the league would sell it for him on its own terms.

His most successful franchise, Hagerstown of the Carolina League, was also experiencing similar problems. Although he was not being forced to sell the Hagerstown club, he had received a substantial offer for the team. Lou needed the money and the offer looked mighty good.

Lou was able to work out an acceptable remedy to the situation in Peoria by securing his own buyer and negotiating a price he could live with. A prominent local businessman, Pete Vonachen, purchased the club and did an outstanding job eliminating problems that he'd inherited. After the sale, Lou moved his Peoria GM, Overstreet, to Jacksonville as sales manager.

Shortly after closing the Peoria sale, Lou decided to sell his most profitable franchise. The Hagerstown staff stayed with the new ownership group.

As the Thanksgiving holiday approached, Bobby Bragan called to let me know he was also having some money problems with Lou. Bobby claimed Lou owed him a fairly substantial amount in back salary and bonuses and wasn't sure they would be able to work things out. Lou was claiming to have no money to pay him, despite having just sold two of his franchises. Bobby informed me that the IRS had taken much of the money to cover non-payment of back taxes.

Bobby was bringing me up to date on the situation and also letting me know that one of the counter offers he was preparing called for Lou to turn the Elmira club over to him as a settlement and buyout of his existing contract. With the financial problems Lou was experiencing, Bobby felt there was a good possibility Lou would accept his offer.

A few days later Bobby called again to inform me that he and Lou had worked out the details and he was now the new owner of the Elmira franchise. We scheduled a news conference and Bobby flew into town to make the announcement.

How quickly things had changed for Lou! Instead of owning five ballclubs with plans to continue growing, he was down to only Jacksonville and Spartanburg. In summary, he had sold Florence, was forced to sell Peoria, sold Hagerstown, and had lost Elmira to settle a bad debt.

Now that the Elmira ballclub was no longer a part of Baseball Enterprises, the nickname Suns was no longer needed. All of Lou's teams carried the Suns nickname because it enabled him to purchase souvenirs for all of the clubs in mass quantities and, frankly, from a business and marketing standpoint, it made a lot of sense.

But the nickname Suns had never been popular in Elmira. The fans were never able to relate to it and it had no real meaning in baseball circles outside of Jacksonville, where the nickname had first been popularized many years earlier. The only nickname that was really accepted in Elmira was the Pioneers, the name the club had been know by before its two seasons of being called the Suns. Changing the nickname back to the Pioneers was the first thing we did after Bobby took ownership. From a public relations standpoint, it was an extremely popular move.

With Bobby as owner, I felt things could only get better. I was a little wary of him but felt much more comfortable than I did working for Lou. One of the first things Bobby did for me when he took ownership was to give me a raise and put it in writing in the form of a contract. It was the first time I had had the security of a written contract and it felt good.

Although it took time to get used to Bobby and the way he did things, the better I got to know him, the more I liked him. He certainly was not without his faults, but when he opened up and let you get to know him, he really was a likeable guy.

His father, Bobby Bragan Sr. is one of the finest gentlemen I have had the pleasure to know. Bobby Sr. played professional baseball for the Phillies and Brooklyn Dodgers before becoming a major league manager for the Pirates, the Indians, and both the Milwaukee and Atlanta Braves. He then went on to become president of the Texas League, then president of The National Association of Professional Baseball Leagues, and followed that by heading up the speakers bureau of the Texas Rangers.

Bobby Jr's uncle, Jimmy Bragan, had played for the Elmira Pioneers in the early 1950s and had a very long tenure as president of the Southern League.

Bobby Jr. was himself an outstanding college player at Mississippi State before signing a pro contract with the Atlanta Braves. He played briefly in their farm system before taking his first administrative job in 1975 as the GM at Class A Harlingen, Texas. The following year he began work in an administrative capacity with the Jacksonville Suns before being named general manager of that Double-A club in '77. Bobby had a solid baseball background as well as strong baseball roots. He taught me a tremendous amount, particularly about stadium operations.

Unlike Lou, he also gave me the authority to hire my own staff, stressing the importance of finding good people that I felt comfortable working with. I decided to bring in an assistant GM and one additional salesperson right after the Christmas holidays.

While I was on a visit to my hometown, Oswego, New York, one weekend, my brother mentioned that he had bumped into an acquaintance of mine, Marty Nash. Marty was also from Oswego and had worked in baseball several years earlier with the Little Falls Mets. He also had worked for the Binghamton Whalers of the American Hockey League. Marty was interested in getting back into pro sports, and although I didn't know him real well, I knew enough about him to feel he probably would fit in nicely with my plans for the upcoming season. So I set up a meeting, decided I felt comfortable with his personality and his work ethic, and offered him the position of assistant GM. He was interested and we came to an agreement.

I also hired Edward "Junior" Irvin, one of the ballpark employees from the previous season, as the additional salesperson. He had been a ticket taker and I had been impressed with his attitude and desire to work in baseball full-time. With our office manager, Jean Hoffman, our staff was now complete.

Marty moved to Elmira to assume his new position on New Year's Day, 1984. On that very day in downtown Elmira at a place called Jones Court, several police officers were shot by several escaped convicts.

Ironically, just a year earlier, when we made our initial move to Elmira, three maximum security prisoners had escaped from the Elmira correctional facility. Not long after, an article in the local paper named the Elmira correctional facility as number one in the state for escapes from a maximum security prison. Every now and then as we looked out our office windows from the ballpark, we would see state police helicopters hovering along the banks of the Chemung River, usually an indication that another prisoner had escaped. After hearing about the shootout on his first day in town, Marty wanted to know what he had gotten into . He really began to wonder about his new position a few days later, when he met John McGovern for the first time.

John was a middle-aged man with a weathered look that made him appear much older than he really was. He also had some difficulty getting around, walking with a pronounced limp. He had been an usher at the ballpark for a number of years and had a tendency to rub fans the wrong way while doing his job. Because it was important to him to be a part of the baseball scene, we were trying to find a position for him where he would do the least damage. He was in the office that morning to discuss just such a move.

With the team changing nicknames, reverting back to the Pioneers, it was only fitting that we develop a new mascot. We dedided John would make a perfect "Elmira Pioneer". In fact, he somewhat looked the part, even without the costume. The expression on Marty's face when, returning to the office after a sales call, he saw McGovern for the first time is hard to describe. I'm not certain if it was disbelief or shock.

McGovern's first question about his new role was who should call the local TV station to line up the interview. I explained the importance of keeping the identity of the mascot a secret, to add to the mystique of the character, similar to that of the famous "San Diego Chicken". He finally agreed to keep quiet about his new alter ego, and our new mascot for the upcoming season was in the fold.

John McGovern was one of the unusual people we encountered during our tenure in Elmira. He loved being around the ballbark. He and his wife Cathy also took on the responsibility of cleaning the stadium after every ballgame, a major undertaking, especially after a big crowd. Fortunately for John, Cathy was not afraid of hard work. Every time we walked through the grandstand while the McGoverns were cleaning, John would stop and strike up a conversation. He looked for any excuse he could find to take a break from his clean-up routine. Many times, while working in our office at the top of the grandstand, we would hear Cathy's shrill voice let out a scream. The first few times we heard her, we ran out to see what all the commotion was about. We'd find Cathy reaming out John for being so lazy. After a while we got used to it, but Cathy continued to do the bulk of the work while John looked for ways to avoid it.

Shortly after the winter weather began to subside, Bobby called from his home in Jacksonville to let us know he was sending a handyman friend of his, Robert Yeargy, to handle routine maintenance around the ballpark. He had worked for Bobby at the ballpark in Jacksonville for years, primarily as a clubhouse attendant and maintenance man. Bobby said Robert would arrive sometime later that day. He had put him on a bus in Jacksonville two days earlier. He told us to let him sleep in the clubhouse until we were able to line up a room for him.

Robert immediately took a liking to John McGovern, who became his stadium assistant. Robert started calling him Waldo. The two of them would walk around the stadium every day, pretending to be busy. Occasionally they would even get some work done.

One of the things Bobby had neglected to tell us was that Robert had a drinking problem. He would be fine until he had some money in his pocket, then would disappear until his money ran out. Then he'd return to work to earn some more money.

The first time Robert disappeared, we were unaware of his problem and had no idea where he was. When Bobby called from Jacksonville to check on him, I explained that we hadn't seen him in a few days. He asked if we had checked the detox unit. I asked Bobby what he was talking about. He explained that it was common in Jacksonville for Robert to go off on a drinking binge, and eventually be picked up and placed in a detoxification cell by the police until he sobered up. So this was our new handyman?

Robert and "Waldo" did accomplish a few things during their rare moments of working together at the ballpark. They built a partition separating the inner and outer offices, but unfortunately, it was not one of Robert's better days. The partition was crooked and unstable and, had the wind been blowing when the door was open, I'm afraid it would have crashed down upon us. The entire partition had to be redone later, after he sobered up.

Another one of Robert's masterpieces was the new cinderblock souvenir stand that he tried to build. He spent weeks laying the blocks, but, when it was all done, the building inspector took one look at it and condemned it as unsafe. The Leaning Tower of Pisa would look upright in comparison. The city then had to knock it down and reconstruct it properly.

The tag team duo of Robert and Waldo struck again several days before the season started. The players had arrived in town and were on the field taking batting practice. Robert and Waldo were repairing a gate on the outfield wall. They had two ladders leaning up against the fence, and Robert was at the top of the ladder on the right. For some reason Waldo was steadying the unoccupied ladder on the left. Robert looked down just as one of the players hit a screaming line drive right at Waldo. Robert yelled "Duck!" Waldo hit the ground, and the ball narrowly missed him. That was the end of Waldo and work for the day, as he immediately retreated to the grandstand.

As the start of the season approached, we had to fire Junior Irvin. One of our advertisers called after we sent him an invoice. He said he had purchased his ad from Junior, and wanted to know why we continued sending him bills when he had already paid. Marty explained that we had no record of payment and asked him to produce the cancelled check, which we saw had been made out to Edward Irvin. The advertiser explained that Junior had told him to make the check out to him personally because it would be easier for him to cash the check and pay the ballclub. I immediately called several other delinquent accounts that Junior had sold and, sure enough, they also had paid Junior directly.

Just as all of the problems with the previous GMs were finally subsiding, along comes Junior. When we confronted him after turning the information over to the local police department, he placed the blame on the previous general manager. That's right! He claimed that Thom Shannon had instructed him to take the money so as to be sure he would get what the club owed him for working. His wife made weekly

*A happy contestant takes a soft drink break with John Pond of P&C Supermarkets and me after competing in our shopping spree promotion on August 14th, 1984.*

payments until she finally covered the debt, to keep him from going to jail.

Despite all these preseason problems, we entered the season with the strongest promotional schedule the club ever had. A major sponsor enabled us to bring in the famous "San Diego Chicken" for the first time. We also scheduled appearances by the Indianapolis Clowns, and Hall-of-Fame pitcher Bob Feller. We planned a T-Shirt Day, a Ball Day, a big July 4th celebration, a sock hop, a supermarket shopping spree, and a used car giveaway.

In fact, the used car giveaway was responsible for another incident during the season, this one involving Bobby Bragan.

*The Beach Boys perform on a stage in centerfield at Elmira's Dunn Field during Labor Day weekend, 1984.*

Bobby had flown to Elmira for the season and did not have a car to drive around town. We had a used car on display in the stadium concourse area to be given away at the end of the season as part of a promotion with a local auto dealership. The car sported a big sign on its roof, letting everyone know the rules on how to win it.

Whenever Bobby needed transportation, he would tell Marty to take the sign off the car and away he would go. It didn't matter to Bobby that the car didn't even have license plates.

One day Bobby decided to drive the car to Syracuse, about 100 miles away. Everything was fine until he returned to Elmira. A police officer stopped him and Bobby called me at home to ask me to come to the ballpark and pick him up. The officer let him off with a stern warning and allowed him to drop off the car at the ballpark. He did not give Bobby a ticket, although he certainly could have. Bobby looked like a youngster who had been reprimanded as I drove him home.

This was just a temporary setback for Bobby. The following day he needed transportation again and, sure enough, he asked Marty to remove the sign once more. We just looked at each other and shook our heads in disbelief. Fortunately, the season was almost over and we would be giving away that car soon, hopefully before Bobby ended up in jail.

Another promotion related incident took place when we held our first ever "Bat Night". To avoid having the bats used as weapons or to destroy ballpark seats, we decided to give them away as the fans left the park after the game rather than as they entered.

The first 1,000 youngsters entering the park were given coupons redeemable for the bats when they exited after the game. Somehow, someone started a rumor early in the game that the bats were being given out and unless you hurried down to the souvenir stand you would miss out.

Standing at the top of the grandstand, I noticed a tremendous number of people heading down the ramps toward the souvenir area. I quickly headed down to see what was going on, why hundreds of people were converging on the souvenir area, where it was beginning to look like a riot.

My wife, who was running the souvenir stand, was standing on a bench trying to calm the swelling mob by explaining that there were plenty of bats for everyone. For a while, I feared for her safety. Eventually we were able to calm the crowd and convince people to return to their seats. It was a scary situation but, fortunately, no one was injured.

Despite all the personnel problems, from a business standpoint, the season was successful. The club finished with a record of 35-38, good for fourth place in the six-team Eastern

*Baseball Winter Meetings, in the Houston Astrodome, December 1984: (from left) Sam and Sue Lazzaro, Pattie and Bobby Bragan.*

Division. Despite the sub .500 record, we set a franchise attendance record by drawing just under 60,000 fans to Dunn Field.

We also placed two players on the post season NY-P All-Star Team, catcher Tony DeFrancesco and pitcher Brad Mettler. Some of the more notable performers in the league were short-stop Kevin Elster of the Little Falls Mets, Jay Buhner of the Watertown Pirates, Lance Johnson of the Erie Cardinals, and Dan Gakeler who pitched for us. Bud Harrelson was named Manager of the Year; he had led the Little Falls Mets to the league title with a play-off victory over the Newark Orioles.

Shortly after the close of the season I was informed by league president Vince McNamara that I had been named the league's Executive of the Year and would receive the award at the Baseball Winter Meetings in Houston in December. Not a bad finish to a strange first year as General Manager. It certainly left me looking forward to the next season.

# 4 The High Roller

Preparing for the 1985 season was relatively calm in comparison to the preceding two. We started planning and working in September, shortly after the close of the 1984 campaign. It felt good not to be mired in major controversy for a change.

All things considered, Bobby had been pretty good to work for, and we anticipated significant revenue growth in the upcoming year. Our greatest concern stemmed from Bobby's unpredictibility. We had no idea what his plans were, but knew him well enough to know that if the right offer for the club came along, he would jump at it.

We had learned enough about Bobby's personal habits, having been around him all season, to know that he loved to gamble. Every home-game night, we each had to throw in a dollar and guess the actual in-stadium attendance. He even required us to do the same whenever we attended a road game together. Gambling appeared to be a real illness.

Once Bobby even had Marty line up a rental car to drive to Atlantic City on an open date. They drove all night to get back on time to prepare for a home game the next day. According to Marty, Bobby would never have left Atlantic City if Marty hadn't threatened to leave without him.

Also, during the off-season, Bobby was calling regularly from his home in Jacksonville to ask how much money we had in the team bank account. Then, he'd instruct me to send portions to him so he could fly to Atlantic City for the weekend. Sometimes we would argue because the balance would get low and we had other obligations to clear up. Occasionally he would listen, but often he insisted that I send him the money. He often used the line that he would send back twice as much on Monday after he won. Never did that actually happen.

Although things continued to go very well, my feeling was that this would probably be my last season working for Bobby in Elmira. I needed more job security than he could offer. One of my biggest concerns was that he might lose the club because of his gambling problem.

During the off-season Bobby negotiated with Lou to buy the Jacksonville franchise. Bobby's uncle, Peter Bragan, was willing to put up the money to purchase the club if Bobby could get Lou to part with it. Bobby believed that if he could get Lou to sell the franchise, Peter would include him as part owner and allow him to operate the club. Lou eventually agreed to the transaction, but to Bobby's surprise, Peter did not include him in the deal. Instead, Peter named Dan Overstreet as his GM and brought in Peter's son to train under him. Bobby was left out in the cold and he wasn't happy with the turn of events.

This left Lou with just one ballclub, Spartanburg. Around this time, he called me to ask if I'd be interested in moving to Spartanburg to run his club. I politely declined, telling him that I was happy with my present situation and had no plans to leave at this point, at least not until after the current season. That was the last time I spoke with him. He passed away several years later.

Despite being cut out of the Jacksonville deal, Bobby still owned Elmira. As the season approached, he made plans to move his wife and daughters to Elmira for the season. They were in the process of selling their Jacksonville home and, for a while, considered buying a home in Elmira. They settled into an apartment complex near the ballpark for the summer, however, while waiting to sell their Florida home.

Shortly before opening day, Dave Wright came to the office to see Marty. Dave was a friend of his in town to interview for the Elmira College soccer coaching position. Dave took the job, and named Marty his assistant, a part-time position that did not conflict with Marty's baseball responsibilities.

Dave's move to Elmira solved another problem for us. During the previous season, John McGovern had not worked out well as the Elmira Pioneer mascot. We were constantly reminding him to keep his head on in public. He'd take the big coonskin-capped papier-maché "pioneer" head off and light up a cigarette whenever he got the urge. The sight of our mascot carrying his head under his arm while smoking could be traumatic for a youngster, especially considering that John looked better with the big, ugly mascot head on. He also didn't get along with the kids. Knowing that he had trouble getting around, many youngsters would pelt him with ice from their drink cups, then run away. John then would wander around the ballpark in search of the young culprits, and on several occasions, I caught him holding a young spectator in a headlock. Our costumed mascot beating up children did little to enhance our image. We considered getting rid of him, but felt sorry for him and understood his desire to be part of the baseball scene.

Late in that season we'd discovered a job he was really cut out for — handling the manually-operated scoreboard that was just above the right centerfield fence. We employed a person to sit on the catwalk under the scoreboard and insert the score each half inning. This person also controlled a set of lights to register balls, strikes, and outs. It worked out perfectly. He was able to work at the park and contribute to the operation, but we were able to keep him away from the fans.

But that meant we needed a mascot, and Dave — young, athletic, and interested — become the Elmira Pioneer. He was popular with the kids and adults, especially the young ladies.

He would encourage the attractive young women to dance with him on top of the dugouts, and he also performed stunts on an all-terrain cycle on the field between innings. It was a tremendous improvement and as Dave gained confidence during the season, he became more creative.

Prior to the start of the '85 season, we secured a new electronic scoreboard as part of a national sponsorship program based on attendance. We became one of the first short season clubs in the country to achieve this distinction. It was a tremendous upgrade for our facility, but it eliminated our new-found position for McGovern.

Regardless of his role, one of the biggest problems we had with McGovern was getting him to stop talking. We finally figured out a way to accomplish this near-miraculous feat. My watch included a stop watch feature, and I would say to John, "Let me time you and see how long you can keep quiet." Before he could respond, I would quickly push the start button on my timer and stare at him. He would immediately stop talking and look at me with a pained expression.

We would continuously challenge him to see if he could break his previous record. He would always fall for it. Even my son, who was now five years old, wouldn't fall for that routine, but it always worked on John.

To cut down on travel and play up geographic rivalries, the New York-Penn League split from two six-team divisions into three divisions of four teams for the '85 season. It really didn't make any difference to our club. We finished dead last in the Central Division with a record of 28-49, 18½ games behind the Auburn Astros, our division winner. Only the Nothern Division's Watertown Pirates (22-54) had a record worse than ours.

The Oneonta Yankees ran away with the Northern Division, finishing 19 games ahead of the runner-up team. They had the best overall record in the league by a considerable margin, and

*The Elmira Pioneer during our Supermarket Shopping Spree at
Dunn Field in Elmira, August 27th, 1985.*

won the year-end play-offs as well. Their manager, Buck
Showalter, was named Manager of the Year.

One of the best players in the league was the center fielder
for the Geneva Cubs, Doug Dascenzo. He hit .333 and stole 33
bases. Jose Mota of the Niagara Falls White Sox hit .303, and
along with Dascenzo was named to the year-end All-Star team.

For the first time in the three seasons I'd been in Elmira, we
placed no one on the year-end All-Star team. Our best pure
hitter was a youngster named Carlos Quintana. He had a beautiful stroke and hit .277 with 4 homers and 35 RBI. We also
had a pretty good defensive center fielder, Brady Anderson,
who hit .256 with 5 homers and led the league with 67 walks.
In addition, one of our catchers was a sixth round draft pick out
of the San Diego area named Todd Pratt. He looked terrible,
hitting only .134 and was very shaky behind the plate. All three
have since played in the major leagues, with Quintana playing
for the Red Sox and Anderson doing very well since coming

over to Baltimore, including a 50 home run season in 1996. Pratt finally made it to "The Show" with the Phillies in 1992.

Despite the horrible record on the field, we shattered our all-time franchise attendance record and led the entire league by drawing 66,636 spectators to Dunn Field.

One of the major promotions for the year was a tie-in with Chemung County and the City of Elmira as they decided to heavily promote a famous son, Samuel Langhorne Clemens, better known as Mark Twain. At the age of 32, in 1867, Clemens had befriended Charles Langdon of Elmira during a Mediterranean cruise and had fallen in love with a miniature portrait of Langdon's sister, Olivia. In 1868 Clemens visited the Langdons and within a year became engaged to Olivia. Sam

*Elmira Pioneers first baseman Tony Scott stretches for the throw as a Watertown Pirates runner races toward the Big Mac during the 1984 season.*

and Olivia were married at the Langdon home on February 2, 1870, and three of their children were born in Elmira.

They spent many summers in Elmira, where Clemens did a lot of writing. A friend of Clemens presented him with a surprise gift in 1874, a study room designed as a replica of a Mississippi steamboat pilot house. Clemens loved it and wrote most of *Tom Sawyer* in the study that summer. After Clemens' death, the Langdon family presented the study to Elmira College, and in 1952 it was completely restored and moved to the college campus, where it is now a popular tourist attraction.

The last summer Clemens spent in Elmira was in 1903. He returned for Olivia's funeral in 1904 and again in 1907 for the dedication of an organ at Park Church. He died in April, 1910, and is buried in Elmira's Woodlawn Cemetery beside members of his family. His family plot is also a popular tourist stop.

"Mark Twain Country" was the theme of the Elmira Chamber of Commerce in 1985, and we also played it up at the ballpark. We had several giveaways of "Mark Twain Country" merchandise during the season, including ball caps, T-shirts, and coffee mugs. We included a story on Mark Twain in our game program as well.

But we had other successful promotions that year, including a return appearance by the "San Diego Chicken", an appearance by Bob Feller, the Indianapolis Clowns comedy barnstorming team, and the "Clown Prince of Baseball", Max Patkin. We featured another "Supermarket Shopping Spree" with contestants again picking up groceries while racing around the bases with shopping carts after a ballgame, a Baseball Card and Memorabilia Show, and a baseball card team set giveaway.

We even scheduled a rain-out as part of our promotional schedule. After having been rained out of our final home game of the season for four consecutive years, we labeled our final home game our "Fifth Annual Season-Ending Rain-Out" and spent all season hyping the fact that we would go ahead with all of our season-ending awards and giveaways, rain or shine.

One of our early-season promotions led to an unusual incident. On "Ball Night", a young fan arrived at the ballpark with a free ticket courtesy of the "Ball Night" sponsor, walked through the gate, collected his free baseball, then headed for the exit. Bobby, who happened to be standing nearby, stopped the youngster at the gate, telling him he couldn't leave with the baseball if he wasn't planning to stay for the game. The youngster handed the ball to Bobby and left the ballpark.

Several minutes later a man charged into the park and started shaking his finger at me, telling me I had no right to take the ball away from his son. At first I couldn't understand what he was talking about, but after he calmed down enough to answer my questions, I understood what had happened and called Bobby over.

They both started talking and, all of a sudden, Bobby pushed the man, got down in a "John L. Sullivan" boxing pose, and said "come on" to him. The man looked totally surprised and immediately stormed out of the ballpark. I was stunned and shaken. I couldn't believe the way Bobby handled the situation. He was all set to square off with the fan in the main entrance area and slug it out in front of a large contingent of fans arriving for the game. All over a free baseball!

I walked out of the stadium into the parking lot to try to collect my thoughts and calm down. Suddenly a car came speeding around the corner, turned into our parking lot almost sideways and, with tires spinning, pulled up to the front entrance and skidded to a halt, almost hitting me.

A woman jumped out of the car and, before I could say anything, she charged up to me, asking, "Are you the man that attacked my husband and son?" I asked her to calm down and tried to explain to her that I wasn't the person she was looking for. Bobby was standing just inside the entrance, and I pointed him out and told her to talk with him.

Bobby also tried to calm her down and offered her two baseballs for her troubles and apologized for losing his cool. She threw the baseballs at Bobby, narrowly missing him and instead hitting his wife Pattie, selling tickets in the ticket booth behind him. Pattie was not seriously injured and the woman then ran out of the park and jumped back in her car, speeding off into the setting sun.

Oh, what fun this game had become! About halfway through the game, as I was making my rounds to check on stadium operations, a police officer walked up to me and asked my name. He said a woman had filed a complaint against me relating to the incident. Apparently she assumed that Bobby was me and had turned my name in to the police.

I tried to explain this to the officer but he continued to ask me to go to the police station with him to answer some questions. Eventually Marty and Bobby joined in the conversation and convinced the officer that I had done nothing wrong. If anything, the woman could have been charged for her erratic behavior behind the wheel, as well as for hitting Patty with the baseballs. The officer finally left, but not before issuing a stern warning about any future behavior of this type.

This was the first of several unbelievable incidents that season involving Bobby. Later, we had an event sponsored by a radio station. The station put together a number of gift packs to be given away via ticket number drawings during the game, and the station manager dropped them off at our office earlier in the day. Bobby went through them and discovered that many contained five-dollar bills along with gift certificates and prize coupons. Bobby helped himself to the five-dollar bills before we were able to give the gift packs away.

After the game, the station manager stopped by the office to check on the prizes. He went through several that had gone unclaimed and discovered the money was missing. He was puzzled. I told him that they had been left on the counter in the office for part of the day and it was possible someone could have gone through the bags. I was certainly telling the truth, as someone had done just that. I wasn't about to get any more specific because I enjoyed my job and wanted to continue working. He shrugged it off, collected the remaining prizes, and away he went.

One other peculiar thing about Bobby was that he used NyQuil regularly for all of his aches and pains. He would take a swig of the medicine every morning to start his day. One night Pattie, arriving alone at the ballpark for the game, reported that Bobby wouldn't be coming because his hernia problem had flared up and he was unable to get out of bed. She said she'd been telling him for years to see a doctor but, instead, when-ever the pain would become unbearable, Bobby would just drink some NyQuil.

Shortly before game time that night, Bobby came strolling into the ballpark. I asked him how he was feeling and he gave me a grin and said, "I'm doin' good" as he patted a bottle of NyQuil that was sticking out of his pocket.

Bobby had also developed another bad habit, one that occurred on a regular basis. His wife Pattie sold tickets at every game, and Bobby made a practice of going into the ticket booth to relieve her each night, waiting until she had built up some cash. He would help himself to some of it to finance his trips to the area horse tracks.

Pattie would get upset with him because she couldn't balance up every night. She complained every time he took over for her. When Bobby got tired of listening to her gripe, he

*Marty Nash,
Bobby Bragan
Jr., and Sam at
the stadium
office at Dunn
Field, Elmira,
in 1985.*

would try to adjust the ticket counts to coincide with the money he took. He was seldom successful.

It didn't take long to figure out what was going on. Every time Bobby went into the ticket booth, we would hear Pattie complain. When she returned to resume her position, Bobby would leave with the same look on his face as the cat that had just swallowed the canary.

Even Bobby's young daughter Brandie had caught on early. She said to Marty one night as Bobby ducked into the ticket booth, "There goes Daddy into Mom's ticket booth to take some money. Mom always gets mad at him because her money doesn't balance at the end of the night. But he doesn't care. We must be going to the track again tomorrow."

During my years in Elmira, our concession operation was handled by a concessionaire, rather than by the club itself. Some clubs prefer to operate their own concessions, feeling it gives them greater quality control and a better opportunity to make money on one of the more profitable avenues available to minor league clubs. Other clubs feel the time and effort required to handle the labor-intensive concession operation can be better spent in other revenue-generating areas, such as group sales and greater promotional involvement.

Plenty of arguments support both theories, so it's really a matter of preference. Under Lou's Baseball Enterprises operation, we worked with an outside concessionaire, who paid the club a flat percentage of the gross concession revenue.

After Bobby took ownership of Elmira, he negotiated his own deal with a local concessionaire. Bobby had problems trusting people, and to forestall any chance of being taken advantage of by an unscrupulous concessionaire, he worked out an arrangement that paid us an agreed-upon amount for each person attending our games.

Because the concessionaire trusted Bobby no more than Bobby trusted him, each designated a person to count people as they entered the park. They also agreed to compromise on any discrepancies.

Bobby usually asked Marty to handle the count, and would constantly tell him to add to his total whenever the concessionaire's counter wasn't looking, and later inform this person that he had missed a few. With Bobby, it was a never-ending battle of trying to get something for nothing by any means possible.

After all, it was Bobby's team, and he could do what he wanted. I can't say that I agreed with everything he did; in fact, when it came to the way he handled the team's finances, I agreed with him very little. He enjoyed playing the role of the well-to-do owner, but he dipped into the till so often and went through the money so quickly that we were often operating from game to game, despite the fact that we were extremely successful and should have been showing a good profit.

Because of the image Bobby tried to convey, Marty secretly dubbed Bobby "the High Roller", and would refer to him by that nickname whenever he wasn't around.

It was also because of these problems that I was bound and determined to break away and find another job with a club offering more stability and security.

# 5  The Triple Move South

The 1985 season finally came to a close. Despite a last place finish our club led the NY-P League in attendance, and we were informed by new league president Leo Pinckney that I would receive the New York-Penn League version of the "Larry McPhail Award for Promotional Excellence". It was pleasing to again be recognized by the league for a successful season, but I was even more determined that the time to make a move was now.

We really didn't want to leave Elmira. We had made some very good friends and things had gone extremely well personally. We had even spent time looking into buying a home there. Both Sue and my son, Sammy, had practically been adopted by the Karam family.

Albert and Sally Karam were two outstanding people. Albert ran a small, corner grocery store and was popular with everyone in town. He was also a Chemung County legislator and a good ally for the ballclub. Sally kept the books for his store. Their son Chris had served as a batboy for the club for many years.

Sally and Sue had become very close. With my grueling schedule of long hours and little time off, it was a real blessing that Sue and Sammy had been able to attach themselves to these fine people. We were really going to miss the Karam's, along with a number of other people we had grown close to. But the overriding factor in the back of my mind was the way

Bobby handled the finances, along with his propensity to gamble.

I began testing the water by calling some contacts made during my three seasons in the game. I talked with the Toronto Blue Jays about several openings that could develop in their farm system. They owned the Class Double-A club in Knoxville and were in the process of buying and operating a New York-Penn League expansion club in St. Catherine's, Ontario. They also were looking at adding a club at their spring training site in Dunedin, Flordia in the near future.

I also talked with the owners of a new expansion franchise scheduled to begin in South Bend, Indiana in the Midwest League in 1987. They were planning to hire their general manager soon to give him plenty of time to put together a staff and build a successful operation while their new stadium was being built. I scheduled an interview with them for early December during the Winter Meetings in San Diego.

Additionally, I was contacted by two individuals interested in getting an Eastern League expansion team for their hometown of Harrisburg, Pennsylvania. I also heard from the prospective new owner of the Salem Redbirds of the Carolina League, who was scheduled to take ownership of that club at the Winter Meetings. I had a full agenda of job possibilities to explore while in San Diego.

My prospects of landing a job with a solid organization looked good. I was comfortable with all the people I was scheduled to interview with, having talked with all of them several times on the telephone. All came across quite well.

South Bend appeared to be a great opportunity, with plans for a new showcase facility in an already sports-crazy market. They had received several hundred resumés for the position and had narrowed their list of potential candidates to eight, all to be interviewed during the Winter Meetings. I was one of the eight finalists.

The two prospective owners of the expansion team in Harrisburg came into Elmira during the season to talk with me about operating a franchise. They also impressed me, but their biggest task in San Diego would be acquiring a team.

The new owner of the Salem franchise was a scouting supervisor for the Montreal Expos named Kelvin Bowles. He had received a glowing recommendation on me from Frank Wren, who had just recently been named the assistant director of scouting for the Expos after operating their New York-Penn League club in Jamestown during the past season. I had helped Frank out whenever he called and apparently he was impressed with the way I handled the daily operations.

I also planned to talk with Gord Ash of the Blue Jays regarding their future opportunities. Overall, I felt good about my chances of finding a new job.

Marty was also interested in making a move. He kept quiet about it, but knew Bobby would not give him the general manager's position if I left. He also intended to keep his eyes and ears open while at the Winter Meetings.

I arrived in San Diego with great anticipation and the interviews went well. The South Bend interview was first, and I felt good about the way things went, with the exception that some very personal and prying questions were asked, which may have overstepped the legal parameters of a job interview, and made me wonder what I could be getting into.

My next interview was with Kelvin Bowles. We failed to make a connection during our first scheduled meeting because the hotel had two separate lobbies and we each went to a different one. But after another phone conversation, we were finally able to get together and talk.

Kelvin was in his mid-forties and had made his mark in the cable television industry in southwest Virginia. His cable success left him financially secure and in a position to purchase the Salem club. He had been a scout for the previous ten years, starting with the major league scouting bureau before moving over to the Pittsburgh Pirates. He had recently left the Pirates to work for the Montreal Expos. Kelvin was born and raised in western Virginia and had bought the Salem club to keep it from leaving the area.

Because of his scouting and numerous other business ventures, Kelvin was looking for a long-term commitment from someone capable of running the entire day-to-day operation. I was impressed with everything he had to say, but the only drawback to this opportunity was that Salem was the same city where I had worked in pro hockey and I wasn't excited about going back again because my hockey experience had left me with a bad taste.

After talks with both the Harrisburg people and Gord Ash from Toronto, I realized there probably would be no opportunity with either of them in the upcoming year. I was left with three possibilities, South Bend, Salem, or stay in Elmira.

I had no intention of making a decision while in San Diego. The South Bend people informed me they would be narrowing down their list after the Winter Meetings concluded. Kelvin was ready to make a commitment, but I told him I'd like to think about his offer until after we returned home. He was willing to give me that much time.

After I returned to Elmira and we carefully weighed the options, we contemplated staying put. But the reasons I wanted to leave Elmira hadn't changed. Also, Bobby had spent nearly all his time in San Diego trying to track down an investor to buy a portion of the team, to give him some operating capital.

Salem seemed to be offering everything that I was looking for, but I couldn't shake that negative image from my hockey experiences.

I received a call from the people in South Bend informing me they were impressed with my interview and I was one of their three finalists. They planned to make a decision soon.

As the Christmas holidays approached, my family and I were still uncertain where we would spend the upcoming season. The office would be shut down for the holidays from the day before Christmas until the day after New Year's Day, so my wife and I decided to take advantage of the time off and travel to Salem to look over the situation and meet again with Kelvin Bowles.

After Christmas with my mother-in-law in Oswego, we left our son behind, and Sue and I journeyed south to the "Friendly City" of Salem, the day after Christmas.

Salem is located in the Roanoke Valley of south-western Virginia, nestled in the Blue Ridge Mountains along the beautiful Blue Ridge Parkway. A hotel room was waiting for us when we arrived after a ten-hour drive.

Up early the next day, we headed to the ballpark office, located next to the stadium in an old City of Salem building, where we met with Kelvin and Jon Kaufman. The city owned the stadium and provided the office as part of the lease with the ballclub, as the old park lacked adequate space.

Jon, originally from Brooklyn, had graduated from Adelphi University four years earlier, where he played a season of baseball. He had also done some baseball and basketball coaching on the amateur level prior to taking the job with the previous owners of the Salem team. Kelvin decided to retain Jon because he had been a great help during Kelvin's negotiations to buy the club. Jon had been the assistant GM, but Kelvin had offered him the title of General Manager to entice him to stay, even though he had already explained to both Jon and myself that I would be responsible for running the club on a day-to-day basis. My official title would be Vice President of Baseball Operations.

We spent several hours with Kelvin and Jon discussing the ballpark, the ballclub, and the complete baseball operation. Then a friend of Kelvin's in the real estate business drove us around the area, showing us homes and apartments. We then went back to the office to talk further with Kelvin and Jon before leaving to meet some friends we had been close to when we lived in the area before.

We took in a lot in a very short time, and our heads were nearly spinning. The underlying impression derived from our day in Salem was the feeling of being wanted. Kelvin really went out of his way to make us feel needed and to explain how important it was to him that I accept the position.

We headed back to Oswego that evening, and during our long drive we talked about the opportunity. The trip had been worthwhile and we made up our minds during the drive that Salem was the place we were going to go. We felt comfortable enough with both Kelvin and Jon to be certain we were making the right move. We also felt there was a tremendous growth potential with the Salem franchise. It would be a real challenge.

My immediate challenge would be finding a way to inform Bobby of my decision to leave Elmira. I would have to do so soon because it was imperative to get back to Salem as quickly as possible to start putting things together for the upcoming season.

Unlike Elmira, Salem is a full-season club, meaning the season opens in early April rather than late June. With Kelvin having just taken over ownership, virtually nothing had been done and we would have less than three months until opening day. On the other hand, Elmira was in great shape. Having been out selling since September, many of our promotional events were already lined up and many more were in the works.

Bobby was back in Jacksonville, having decided that the Elmira winter was a little too cold for him. He'd just learned that his uncle had decided not to bring Dan Overstreet back to run the Jacksonville club, and Bobby, who'd always been high on big Dan, wanted to hire him in some capacity. So, when I broke the news to Bobby about my leaving, I reminded him that Dan was available to step right in. I offered to stick around long enough to help Dan get started.

Bobby accepted the idea and decided that he and Dan would head up in the next few days. In the meantime, Marty informed me that he had been contacted by Miles Wolff. Miles had just been granted an expansion franchise in the Appalachian Rookie League to be located in Burlington, North Carolina. He wanted Marty to become his GM, and Marty had already accepted the position. He would start his new job in mid-January.

I've already mentioned Miles Wolff, the owner of the Utica Blue Sox. Most baseball insiders know Miles Wolff, whose involvement in the ownership end of pro baseball began in 1980 when he borrowed some money from friends and relatives and started up an expansion franchise in the Carolina League. And, as they say, the rest is history.

The Carolina League team was the Durham Bulls. The Bulls exceeded even Wolff's greatest expectations, becoming one of the most successful franchises in the minor leagues. After the 1991 season Wolff sold the Bulls for a figure reported in excess of $4 million.

Wolff has been involved in the ownership of several other minor league clubs over the years and is also owner and publisher of *Baseball America*, one of the major baseball news publications. Since selling the Bulls, Wolff has remained active in the game, and was heavily involved in the 1993 start-up of the independent Northern League in the upper midwest, and currently serves as Northern League President/Commissioner.

Coincidentally, Dave Wright, our team mascot, had also accepted a new position. He was leaving his full-time soccer coaching job at Elmira College to accept a similar position with Gettysburg College in Gettysburg, Pennsylvania.

Ironically, all three of us were heading south at around the same time. We decided to coordinate our trips. We rented a large truck and made the move together, planning to stop in Gettysburg first, then Salem, and finally ending the journey in Burlington, moving north to south.

On Friday evening, January 10th, we loaded Marty's belongings first, following the packer's motto FILO (first in, last out). Early Saturday morning we assembled at my apartment, as we would be second to unload and last, we loaded Dave's items, as he would exit first.

We had a crisp, clear, beautiful day for traveling and our journey went well. Our first problem occured when we arrived at the Gettysburg address Dave had listed for his new residence. It was an apartment building, but apparently Dave's prospective new landlord knew nothing about Dave's scheduled arrival.

After a great deal of discussion, things were resolved and we unloaded Dave's belongings. We then continued on our way south. We arrived in Salem around nine p.m. and went straight to the apartment complex that Jon Kaufman had lined up for us.

We unloaded my belongings and, with things strewn all around the apartment, slept on the floor in sleeping bags and blankets that first night. The following morning, I continued down to Burlington with Marty. We left the rental truck at the Burlington Holiday Inn, and Marty drove me back to Salem.

# 6 Can't Anybody Here Play This Game?

The triple move south was complete. I was in Salem and ready to go. We had less than three months to put everything together for our April opener. I don't think I've ever worked as long and hard. Jon and I put in at least twelve hours a day, seven days a week, for three consecutive months. I hardly saw my wife and son. There was so much to do and so little time to do it.

To further complicate matters, the local economy was strained. Less than two months earlier, a devastating flood had hit the Roanoke Valley, causing millions of dollars in damages and knocking a number of companies out of business.

There were also a number of negatives affecting the club. Name recognition was extremely low for a team that has been in existence for so many years, and the ballpark was old and badly in need of renovation. A high turnover rate of front office personnel had also contributed to a serious lack of consistency in dealing with the public, prospective sponsors, and advertisers. In addition, our club had never been marketed properly, and we spent much time trying to educate the public as to who we were and what we had to offer.

Kelvin had just become the third club owner in five years. He had purchased the club to make sure it stayed in Salem after the previous owners, Arthur Hecht and Stan Waldshan had first threatened, then attempted, to move it to Charleston, West Virginia. They decided to sell after the league voted against their attempted move.

One of the most important things Kelvin had mentioned to me with regard to accepting the Salem position was that he was looking for a commitment from someone interested in staying with the club for a long time. It wasn't hard to understand why.

Even the club nickname, Redbirds, seemed inappropriate. Everyone thought the club was affiliated with the St. Louis Cardinals, but our parent club was the Texas Rangers. The nickname had come about as the result of a name-the-team contest held in 1980, after Larry Schmittou purchased the club and decided the Pirates moniker was not as marketable as establishing a separate identity from the parent club, which was the Pittsburgh Pirates at that time. This theory is solid, but the nickname Redbirds did little to serve that purpose. After the 1980 season, Schmittou severed ties with the Pirates and brought in the San Diego Padres. The Padres remained in Salem in '81 and '82, then shared a working agreement with the Texas Rangers in '83. In 1984 Texas assumed the full working agreement, signing a three-year player development contract that committed them to Salem through 1986.

Another negative problem during my first year was that Texas was planning to sever ties with us after the '86 season, and we had no other major league team showing any interest in coming into Salem. The public perception of the team seemed very negative as well. Nearly everyone mentioned how bad the team was. We really had our work cut out for us.

Despite all of the negatives, we tried to play up the positives. Contrary to popular belief, the club had the second-best record in the Carolina League in '85, trailing only the Lynchburg Mets. The team also could boast of having an all-star at second base in Jerry Browne. Paul Kilgus and Mitch Williams pitched for the '85 Redbirds.

In the business of public relations, perception is everything. Our greatest task was to change that perception from negative

*Rocky the Redbird (left), a favorite with the youngsters.*

to positive. We started by issuing news releases on a regular schedule, digging up every tidbit of positive information that we could find. Each release was built around some positive aspect. Even when the team played poorly, you could often find a silver lining. A hitting streak, spectacular defensive play, or just about any positive player accomplishment gave us a base to build each release around, then we filled it with information on promotional events and sponsorships.

We also began trying to put as many media people as possible into our scheduled events. We instituted a media luncheon to introduce our players at the start of the season, and followed up with additional media gatherings for every major promotional event. We brought in celebrity softball teams and pitted them against local media teams in exhibition games prior to our regular league contests. We let media people hit against Bob Feller during his appearance prior to one of our games.

Different radio stations sponsored nights at the ballpark with ticket giveaways over their airwaves, and appearances by their on-air-personalities. These people could get the word to the public much more effectively than we could, so we made it a point to play up the positives with these people whenever we could. It seemed to be working.

By the time the season was over, the public perception had changed dramatically. We were stunned! People who wouldn't have given us the time of day prior to the season, were now raving about what a great year it had been. What made these comments even more incredible was the fact that our club lost 93 games! It was one of the worst records in the minor leagues. In fact, only one team in all of pro baseball had a worse record, the Texas Rangers' other advanced "A" club, Daytona Beach (40-97) of the Flordia State League.

Our '86 Redbirds were certainly one of the worst pro clubs imaginable. With an overall record of 45-93, they finished dead last in the league. The Carolina League plays a split schedule, meaning we play two 70-game halves. The nice thing about it is if you start off poorly and have a bad first half, there is always the second half to look forward to, when every club starts over at 0-0.

In 1986 it didn't matter. The club finished a distant last in the first half. Then, after opening the second half with three straight wins, proceeded to sink into the basement once more, again finishing the second half on the bottom.

Our club finished next to last in the league in team batting average and home runs, despite the fact that our home ballpark, Municipal Field, was one of the best parks for hitters in all of baseball. With very short dimensions down the lines, 316 feet in left and 302 in right, the park also has virtually no power alleys. Both right and left field power alleys measure about 323 feet from home plate, and although it is 408 feet to dead center field, the ball also carries very well there. A team that has poor offensive numbers when playing all their home games in our park, is definitely a poor-hitting team.

Unfortunately, the hitting was outstanding compared to the pitching. Our pitching staff had the highest team ERA in the league by a considerable margin, at 5.60, and also finished last in complete games with only five and in shutouts with just two. Had it not been for a pretty good relief pitcher, Gary Mielke, who joined us late in the season, we would also have finished last in the league in saves.

Surprisingly, six members of that club went on to play in the major leagues. It just goes to show that you can never be totally certain of anything in this game. As bad as the '86 club performed, it is hard to imagine anyone on the team making "The Show".

Our leading home-run hitter was Kevin Reimer, an outfielder/first baseman/designated hitter, with 16. Kevin had several pretty good seasons in the big leagues before moving on to play in Japan. Our catcher, Chad Kreuter, hit only .220 with six homers but has also done fairly well as a major league performer.

Four pitchers from that team have gone on to the big leagues. Randy Kramer pitched for a while with the Pittsburgh Pirates, and Mielke, our ace stopper, played for several major league clubs. John Barfield and Kenny Rogers have both pitched for the Texas Rangers, with Rogers throwing a perfect game for the Rangers in 1994. Rogers moved to the New York Yankees in 1996.

One of the players who had a less-than-impressive season was Bruce Williams, brother of Mitch "Wild Thing" Williams. Mitch had had control problems while pitching for Salem the previous season, but they were mild compared to Bruce's. Bruce had come over from the Brewers' organization. In 31 innings, he allowed 50 hits, walked 51, and posted a 14.23 ERA. We had several others with numbers nearly as bad.

Overall, the league was strong. The Hagerstown club had a number of veterans, including several with major league experience, along with several of the top prospects in the league. This combination enabled Hagerstown to post the best overall record, along with an incredible league-leading .290 team batting average. They also finished first in both halves in the Northern Division.

They placed three players on the season-ending league All-Star team: second baseman Pete Stanicek, third baseman Craig Worthington, and outfielder Sherwin Cijntje. Former big leaguers Dan Norman, Ted Wilborn, and Glenn Guliver also played for this Baltimore Orioles affiliate.

The Winston-Salem Spirits finished with the second-best overall record, winning both halves in the Southern Division. They were led by All-Star outfielder Doug Dascenzo, catcher Hector Villanueva, and pitcher Dave Pavlas, along with Manager-of-the-Year Jim Essian.

The Player of the Year in the Carolina League in '86 was Gregg Jefferies of the Lynchburg Mets. Jefferies led the league in hitting with a .354 average, along with 11 homers, 80 RBI, and 43 stolen bases. Dascenzo finished second with a .327 mark, followed by teammate Villanueva at .318. Stanicek not only hit .317 but stole 77 bases.

The league's top double-play combination belonged to the Durham Bulls, with shortstop Jeff Blauser and second baseman Ronnie Gant. Gant had a tremendous season, hitting .277 with a league-leading 26 home runs and 102 RBI. He also stole 35 bases. In addition, the Bulls' outfielder, Dave Justice, hit .279 with 12 homers and 44 RBI in only 67 games.

Prince William Pirates pitcher John Smiley had a good season out of the bullpen, posting 14 saves and being called up to the major leagues with the parent Pittsburgh Pirates in September. Smiley has since become a successful starting pitcher on the big-league level.

In the play-offs, heavily favored Hagerstown fell to Winston-Salem, three games to one, giving the Spirits their second consecutive league title.

It was a season filled with unusual events in Salem. One of the highlights was the amazing working relationship we had with our field manager, Mike Bucci. Bucci was somewhat of a "wheeler-dealer", but he also realized that the more he was able to do for the front office, the more he would get from us in terms of special favors. Never before or since have I worked with a field manager as cooperative.

Bucci had begun his managerial career two years earlier with the Sarasota Rangers Gulf Coast rookie league club. He advanced the following season to the Texas Rangers Class A Midwest League team in Burlington, Iowa. He played in both the Rangers and Cleveland Indians farm systems, advancing as high as Triple-A, with his best season being 1978, when he hit .331 with 21 stolen bases as an All-Star third baseman for Tucson.

The weather in southwest Virginia can be fickle in April and it was 28 degrees at game time on April 22, with snowflakes blowing in a strong northwesterly wind, creating a wind chill well below zero. Bucci pleaded with me to cancel the game; it didn't take much for him to win his case. We had a grand total of one fan in the seats, long-time season-ticket holder Robley Stearnes. Stearnes was doing his best imitation of a Green Bay Packer fan, buried in heavy winter gloves, boots, and a hooded snorkel parka.

Bucci had assured me that if I canceled the game, they would play a doubleheader the following night regardless of the weather. He kept his word and we played two games the next

*Salem Redbirds Manager Mike Bucci being introduced to the media prior to the 1986 season.*

night in the bitter cold, with just over 100 fans in attendance. Players were burning old bats in the dugouts and bullpens in an attempt to get warm. Less than a dozen fans stayed until the end as we got hammered in both games by Hagerstown. To reward their loyalty, we gave free tickets to the following game. Actually, those who went home early got the better deal, as we got hammered again the following night.

Also early in the season, Stearnes, well known for his loud heckling, began to get to Bucci. Stearnes had become quite loud and was extremely critical of our manager and players nearly every night.

One night, right after our team finished going through its pre-game infield ritual, Bucci came up in the stands and started talking to Stearnes. After a few minutes, Stearnes followed Bucci from the grandstand into our team clubhouse.

Just before game time, Stearnes, who was in his late 60s, came walking out of our clubhouse wearing a complete team uniform and went into our dugout with Bucci. When we came up to hit in the bottom of the first, Stearnes trotted out to the first base coaching box. Bucci had made him a coach for the night, and he was having the time of his life. His heckling subsided considerably from that point on, as he came away

*Mike Bucci*
*in the dugout.*

with a whole new respect for the players and manager and what they were trying to accomplish on the field. It didn't hurt Bucci's cause when a number of our regular fans returned the favor and heckled Stearnes each time he trotted out to the first base coaching box.

Another unusual event that took place during the season was a try-out camp for the Texas Rangers conducted by Bucci on August 9th. One of the people who came out for the camp was also a season-ticket holder of ours named Ron Gilley. He was a little older than most of the other aspiring big leaguers and not in the greatest physical shape.

When all the other players began stretching and getting loose, Gilley warmed up by sitting down on a bench outside the clubhouse and smoking a cigarette. Bucci had all the patience in the world when it came to dealing with the public, and he treated Gilley as if he were a legitimate prospect, even though it became apparent early that he wasn't.

Surprisingly, during the fielding portion of the try-out, Gilley went to the shortstop position to take ground balls. Even more surprising was that he was able to get to every ball hit to him, although his throwing arm left much to be desired.

When it was time for him to hit, he stepped into the batter's box on the right hand side of the plate and took his ten swings. Jon Kaufman, who was helping Bucci with the camp, was on the mound pitching. He was just laying the ball into the strike zone to see what the hitters could do with it, but Gilley was able to foul off only one pitch during his ten cuts.

After he finished, Gilley then announced that he would take ten more from the opposite side of the plate and stepped over into the lefthander's box. He feebly waved at his ten pitches from that side of the plate also. Bucci then looked at Kaufman and said, "Switch hitter, make a note of that."

Finally, they lined up all the players to time them in the 60-yard dash. As Gilley sprinted toward the finish line, his keys flew out of his pocket. He immediately stopped and began searching around in the grass until he found them, then continued to the finish line. Even if he hadn't stopped for his keys, it's unlikely he would have set any speed records. But Bucci took it all in stride, never once making him feel out of place.

One of the pitfalls of being in pro baseball is the lack of time one is able to spend with friends and family. On the road nearly half the time, players and coaches find it tough to live a normal family life. Bucci decided to make the most of the time he had to spend with his wife Lisa and two young sons, Tony and Carmine.

Late in the season, he decided to take his family camping. Unlike normal families with time off for summer vacations, baseball managers have to be at the park every day for games. So Mike decided to set up his tent inside our ballpark, in a grassy area behind our grandstand. Mike, Lisa and the two boys spent the entire seven-day homestand living in the tent inside the ballpark. Bucci certainly deserves credit for making the most of the situation.

Another thing that he deserves credit for also occurred late in the season. Mike was having trouble with one of the umpires and had been ejected by that umpire during a recent road trip. The same umpire was working the plate on this particular evening in our ballpark and made a call that Bucci vehemently disagreed with.

Bucci went out to the plate and began arguing with this umpire. Suddenly he stopped in mid sentence and demanded that the umpire "Wait right here!" He then ran over to the grandstand fence near the home dugout where his wife was sitting and called to her. He told her to take the two boys and leave the ballpark immediately. She hurriedly followed his instructions and as they left, Bucci ran back to finish his conversation with the umpire.

He knew he was about to lose his cool but had the presence of mind not to do so in front of his wife and two young sons. As soon as they were out of earshot he really tore into the umpire verbally, making sure he got his money's worth before being ejected from the game. It was an amazing performance.

Earlier in the season, he had put on another outstanding performance for us. It was mid-May and we had the San Diego Chicken in town for our game that night. It had rained all afternoon, and we feared the worst. The field had been covered all during the rain and was in pretty good condition. By game time, the rain had stopped, but the damage had been done. The crowd had been scared away by the afternoon showers and, if we played the game, we would lose our shirts financially.

The San Diego Chicken is one of the biggest draws in all of pro baseball. However, he doesn't come cheap and, once he starts his performance, he is entitled to his full appearance fee. We were in a bind. If the field were unplayable, we would have to pay the Chicken only a portion of his fee and could reschedule him at a later date and take our chances on better weather.

Bucci came up with a solution. He had me walk onto the field with him at game time and lift up sections of the tarp which was still covering the infield. As I lifted each section just high enough for him to look under, he would shake his head dejectedly to signify the field was unplayable.

It worked! Everyone was convinced the field was in such bad condition that we couldn't play. We were able to reschedule the Chicken at a later date. We had beautiful weather the second time around, and a large crowd was in attendance.

One other thing that stood out about Bucci was his ability to solve his own problems. When he didn't like the condition of the playing field, rather than complain, he would come out to the park early and grab a rake and rework it until he was satisfied. We would often see Bucci mowing the grass to be sure it met his specifications.

With our short fences and non-existent power alleys, we were always running out of batting practice balls. Bucci would work out deals with the kids in the neighborhood to get them to return the balls that they collected in their yards. One of the best baseball trades ever occurred when he traded an autographed picture of the San Diego Chicken to a neighborhood youngster for two shopping bags full of baseballs.

*A familiar face at Municipal Field. The Kool-Aid Man stops by for a ballgame during 1986 season.*

Speaking of the San Diego Chicken, following the cancellation of his first appearance, many of our players celebrated their night off with a party in the clubhouse after everyone else had left the stadium. We had a pitcher who had just turned 19 and was taking a lot of friendly jibing from his teammates because he had never been with a woman. Several players felt it was time to rectify the situation and drove to an area in nearby Roanoke where they "hired" two women to bring back to the party to teach our young pitcher the ropes. Another pitcher utilized the team videocamera to document the event.

The following day, Bucci walked into the clubhouse and found the players gathered around the TV set, watching the highlight tape from the party. He immediately confiscated the tape, much to the disappointment of the players.

In a season filled with unusual events, one took place in our press box. Our official scorer, Brian Hoffman, is the Sports Editor of *The Salem Times-Register*, a local weekly newspaper. Brian has been the official scorer for years and is one of the easiest people in the world to get along with. On the other hand, our beat reporter that year for the daily newspaper, *The Roanoke Times & World News*, was Bob Teitlebaum. Teets, as he is known by most people, can be very difficult to get along with. He is opinionated and loves to argue with anyone and everyone who will give him the opportunity.

Brian and Bob are good friends and have known each other for years. But one night in the press box, they got into an argument over their rotisserie league teams, and things really became heated. Eventually they began shouting at each other so loud that the batter stepped out of the batter's box and the home plate umpire called time, because everyone in the infield had stopped to look up to see what was going on. Brian ended up throwing a chair across the press box at Teets before storming out to finish scoring the game while seated in the stands.

While we are on the topic of Bob Teitlebaum, let me tell you about his wife. Binki Teitlebaum is a real baseball fan and attends more games than her sportswriter husband. She also liked to find things to complain about, and seemed especially critical in 1986. Maybe the ballclub's record had something to do with it, but it got to a point where it began to get on everyone's nerves.

One of the things that upset us most was that she would go to the ticket window and complain to our ticket sellers about selling the seat next to hers. Here we were, struggling to turn around a previously unsuccessful franchise and she was complaining because we had sold that ticket. If she didn't want anyone in that seat she should have purchased the ticket herself.

We decided to give her something to complain about. We had a fan who would show up on a regular basis in a state of intoxication. He would always try to get us to give him a free beer and we decided to strike a deal with him. We would buy him his first beer every night, and let him sit in one of the best seats in the house, providing he would sit there for the entire game. He agreed and we put him in the seat right next to Binki.

Needless to say, she wasn't at all amused by his presence. He would chain smoke, blowing smoke in her face and drink until we would cut him off each night. After several nights we decided we had punished her enough. We felt that anyone we sold that ticket to in the future would be a definite improvement from what she had just endured and she might stop complaining. It didn't work though.

Later that same season, the inebriated fan came up to the stadium gate complaining that a car had chased him around the parking lot and run over him. Although the top of his head was bleeding slightly, the injury looked mild for someone who claimed a car had just run completely over the top of him three times. We offered to call for medical help, but he refused and went in to watch the ballgame. We surmised that, in the condition he was in, he probably had fallen and hit his head. But he insisted, and seemed to sincerely believe that a car had run over him.

To further complicate matters during the season, we also went through several groundskeepers. As we were to find out in the years to come, this situation was not all that uncommon. Our first groundskeeper had taken on the added responsibility of cleaning the stadium after each home game. This was a major task, requiring a great deal of time and effort.

Late one afternoon during the middle of a homestand, Jon came into the office to tell me that the stadium had not yet been cleaned and our groundskeeper was nowhere to be found. With a ballgame just several hours away, Jon and I grabbed shovels and brooms and began hurriedly cleaning the stadium. We called in an employee who knew a little about preparing the field, and were able to get everything ready on time.

Later that evening, our groundskeeper's wife called to inform us that her husband was in jail for assault. He had gotten into an argument with his landlord and hit him. During the several days before he was released, Jon and I, along with several stadium employees, handled the groundskeeping and clean up. So you want to work in baseball, huh?

We had a home game scheduled on the Fourth of July, during the afternoon. As game time approached, our groundskeeper, Kaufman, and Bucci were standing at the base of our flagpole in center field. Bucci had a fishing pole in his hand and appeared to be casting it up in the air.

Somehow, after the flag had been removed the night before, the rope that is used to raise it had been pulled to the top of the pole and was stuck there. Because it was a holiday, no one from the city with a bucket truck was available to help us out.

Bucci was using his fishing pole to try and hook onto the rope and pull it down. He was not having much success so we needed an alternate plan.

Since it was the Fourth of July, we decided to have our batboys present the colors at home plate as part of a special pre-game ceremony, in which they walked to home plate holding the flag while the National Anthem played. Everything came off without a hitch. It looked like it had been our plan all along.

Despite the weak ballclub, we had a very good season from a business standpoint. We had a promotional event of some type nearly every night. In addition to the San Diego Chicken, we also brought in Bob Feller, Max Patkin, and the touring softball team, The Queen and Her Court. Appropriately, Marvelous Marv Throneberry made an appearance. His experience with the '62 Mets made him feel right at home with our last-place club.

We also had a number of souvenir giveaways, including poncho night, pennant night, bat night, jacket night, beach bag night, baseball card night, cap night, and team photo night.

We worked with an outside telemarketing firm for the first time, allowing them to sell discounted tickets for a game in exchange for a percentage of the proceeds. They were extremely successful, selling more than 28,000 tickets for the June 9th "School's Out" event. We had no idea what kind of return we would get on the tickets as the night approached.

Over 6,600 people attended. The only thing that enabled us to accommodate them all in our park, in which we are barely able to squeeze 5,000, was the fact that as people continued to arrive throughout the early innings, nearly as many were leaving due to the performance of our ballclub on the field!

We were playing Hagerstown. Their first baseman, Dave Falcone, set a new Carolina League record by driving in eleven runs with two grand slams and a three-run homer in his first three trips to the plate. The Suns had jumped to an 11-0 lead in the top of the first inning and never looked back, en route to a 21-3 victory. The only suspense that kept some of the fans around was whether or not Falcone would hit another home run. Not surprisingly, he hit the ball harder his fourth time up than when he'd homered in his previous three trips to the plate. This time, however, his screaming liner was caught by our leaping center fielder, Dan Van Cleve, in front of the wall in dead center field.

Crowds like this contributed to our success. Even though the club was never very competitive, we were able to draw more than 87,000 fans for the season, the second highest total in franchise history. Just further proof that, regardless of how the team plays, you can still operate successfully. Had it not been for some bad weather late in the summer, we probably would have broken the all-time franchise attendance record of 102,456.

As the season was winding down, I received another phone call from the people in Harrisburg. It appeared likely they would finally get the opportunity to put an Eastern League club there and were interested once again in talking with me about running it for them.

I informed them that I had accepted the position in Salem with the understanding that I would give it at least two seasons, so I was already committed for '87. They wanted to talk anyway.

I was planning a trip to Hampton that weekend to see our club take on Peninsula. I had not yet seen the Peninsula ballpark and was looking forward to spending the day at Virginia Beach with my wife and son before heading out to the game that night.

I agreed to meet with Brad Shover and Jeff Kurkis that morning at our hotel. I talked with them for several hours, offering them advice and counseling on every aspect of running a club that I could think of. Before our meeting ended, they offered me a contract with a higher base salary than I was currently making, along with extensive benefits, including profit sharing and pension plans, which at the time few minor league executives received.

I've always believed that a person is only as good as his word, and mine had already been given to Kelvin. I again turned down their offer.

It was fortunate that I did, because at the Winter Meetings later that year in Hollywood, Florida, they were again denied their franchise. This time it appeared they would end up in court, claiming they had reached agreement to purchase an

existing franchise and move it to Harrisburg. The current owner
then backed out of the sale, electing to move the club to Harrisburg himself. Shortly thereafter, Shover and Kurkis did purchase the Spartanburg club in the South Atlantic League.

As the current season was coming to a close, the biggest
question we had to face was who would become our new major
league parent club in '87.

Texas had already informed us that they would be leaving
after the season. We had talked with Boston, Toronto, the New
York Yankees, Seattle, and Cleveland. None had shown much
interest. The biggest problem we were running into in securing
a new working agreement was our facility. Our old ballpark,
with cinderblock outfield walls, light poles on the playing field,
inferior clubhouses, and substandard outfield dimensions, was
a definite handicap.

Texas was leaving to concentrate their advanced "A" efforts
in a new facility scheduled to be built in Port Charlotte,
Florida. Other clubs were being courted by cities interested in
building beautiful new stadiums in order to lure a professional
franchise.

Municipal Field in Salem had first been laid out in 1927,
when Calvin Coolidge was in the White House and Babe Ruth
was embarking on his record-setting 60-home run season. In
fact, "The House that Ruth Built", Yankee Stadium, had
opened only four years earlier. Surprisingly, some of the seats
from Yankee Stadium found their way to Municipal Field in the
late 1950s.

In 1939 Municipal Field had been literally turned around,
and the dugouts and two sections of cement bleachers were
constructed. The "Salem Friends" of the Virginia State League
played there from 1939-42 but folded during World War II. The
Roanoke Red Sox then emerged at Maher Field in Roanoke as

the pro baseball team of the Roanoke Valley, and Municipal Field remained virtually unchanged until the mid 1950s.

After the demise of the Roanoke Red Sox in 1953, the valley was left without a pro baseball team until the Salem Rebels entered the Appalachian League in 1955. The Rebels finished in first-place with a club that won 84 and lost only 38. However, the full-season Appy League then folded. It re-emerged as a short season (70 games) rookie league in 1957, with Salem remaining a member through '67.

During this time, the ballpark was dramatically improved. A scoreboard was added, several more sections of concrete bleachers were poured, and the seats that had once been in Yankee Stadium were purchased from a Yankee farm club located in Schenectady, New York that had folded. The clubhouse was built and lights were installed.

In 1968 Salem stepped up to the full-season Carolina League and has remained a member ever since. In '85 a new scoreboard was installed, and new lights were added prior to the '87 season. But overall, compared to the wave of beautiful new ballparks popping up all around the country, Municipal Field left a great deal to be desired, and this was reflected in the lack of interest shown by major league clubs as we were seeking an affiliation.

Finally, as September approached, we received some positive news. A major league club was interested in coming to Salem, and Kelvin had already worked out the details. We scheduled a news conference to make the announcement.

# 7 The Bucs are Back — and How !

Branch Rickey, III, the farm director of the Pittsburgh Pirates, arrived in Salem on September 2nd for the news conference to announce that the Pittsburgh Pirates were returning to Salem after a six-year absence. The Pirates had been affiliated with Salem for 17 consecutive years, starting with the rookie Appalachian League in 1964.

When Salem had first entered the full-season Carolina League in '68, it was as a Pirates affiliate. The Pirates remained a part of Salem baseball until the conclusion of the '80 season, when owner Larry Schmittou decided the Pirates had not been competitive enough in Salem and made a change.

The six seasons without the Pirates had been mediocre at best. In fact, several of the teams had been just plain horrible. The '82 team posted a record of 39-101. In '83 the team improved to 50-89. Not much to brag about.

On the other hand, the Pirates could boast of a long and rich tradition in Salem. Many of the members of the '79 Pittsburgh World Championship club had played in Salem, including Dave Parker, John Candelaria, Ed Ott, Kent Tekulve, Rennie Stennett, and Omar Moreno.

Other Pirates stars of the recent past had also made their marks in Salem, including Bob Robertson, Dave Cash, Richie Hebner, Richie Zisk, Tony Pena, and Ed Whitson. Many local fans had been upset when the Pirates were forced out of Salem after the '80 season, and the lack of success of both San Diego and Texas affiliates had only made things worse.

Even though the Pirates were struggling on the major league level, having finished last in the National League East (64-98 in '86), they appeared to be an organization on the rise. Syd Thrift had recently taken over as senior vice president and general manager and they had called up one of their best minor league prospects during the previous season, a player named Barry Bonds. Bobby Bonilla had also been re-acquired from the Chicago White Sox in late July, and they would acquire a pitcher named Doug Drabek from the Yankees in November. In addition, they had hired a young manager named Jim Leyland from the White Sox organization prior to the '86 season.

The pieces were being assembled for a club that would soon challenge for the division title. The farm system was also starting to blossom, and a number of good young players were already under contract. Added to the long and rich Pirates tradition in Salem, things were suddenly looking pretty good for us. A month earlier we had no idea whether we would even have a major league affiliate in '87, and here we were announcing a four-year agreement with the Pirates, which would take us through the 1990 season.

On October 1st, 1986, almost exactly one month after announcing our re-affiliation with Pittsburgh, we officially changed our team nickname to the Buccaneers. In the seven seasons that the club had been known as the Redbirds, the name had never really caught on in the community. The name had also become synonymous with losing teams.

By adopting the Buccaneers' nickname and designing a new logo, we were able to establish our own identity, even though the connection with the Pirates was obvious. We also replaced our colors of white with red and blue trim with the Pirates' colors of white with black and gold.

Just before the Thanksgiving holiday, we were informed that our field manager for the upcoming season would be Steve

Demeter. Demeter had played briefly in the major leagues, for the Detroit Tigers in 1959 and the Cleveland Indians in '60, but the majority of his playing career had been spent at the Triple-A level. In fact, he had been named the greatest third baseman in Rochester Red Wings history.

Steve was the Pirates' field coordinator in 1986 after having served as a major league coach with the Pirates the previous season. He had also been their minor-league hitting instructor from 1981 until he became a big league coach in '85. Demeter had already spent three seasons managing in Salem, first in 1973, then in '76, and again in '77. From 1978-80 he managed the Pirates Double-A club. It was obvious we were getting a manager with tremendous experience and knowledge.

Prior to the start of the season, a number of renovations were made at Municipal Field. A completely new lighting system was installed, bringing our lights from one of the worst in the league to one of the best. We had also worked out an arrangement with the city to expand the home clubhouse by adding a new trainers' room and manager's office.

Just as the season got under way, several days of heavy rains caused some flooding in the Roanoke area. The weather was interfering with our home schedule, but the worst was yet to come. The trainer in the clubhouse called the office to inform us that the walls on the newly built trainers' room and manager's office were leaking and they were moving all of their equipment. A short while later the walls caved in. We had a real mess on our hands. With the season already underway, it was a real inconvenience to call the contractor back to rebuild the new clubhouse additions that had just been completed.

We were able to survive this ordeal, but shortly thereafter the city brought in a load of infield dirt to fill in the low spots that develop over time. Unfortunately, no one from the ballclub was present when they dumped the dirt. It appeared that it came from a landfill. Broken glass, rocks, tree limbs, nuts and bolts, spark plugs, and a number of other things that don't belong on a pro baseball field, were mixed with the infield dirt.

Our team was ready to work out. Buzzy Keller, the Pirates' field coordinator, was in town to see the club. He couldn't believe his eyes. Luckily, we were able to get a city work crew to rush over to begin picking up the garbage and trash that was mixed in with the dirt. They removed many of the larger items before we had to prepare the field for the game that night.

The following morning we had the entire infield dirt scraped out and replaced, but this time we made sure we had plenty of people inspecting the new dirt, and, when necessary, sifting it before putting it down. Incredibly, the same thing happened a few weeks later when the city again dropped several truckloads of bad dirt when no one was around, and we had to go through the same process all over.

We had some outstanding talent on that '87 club. Jeff King, the first player selected in the '86 draft out of the University of Arkansas, started the season as our third baseman. A shoulder injury forced Demeter to move him to first base to keep his potent bat in the line up. Steve Moser had a solid season at second base both offensively and defensively.

Our shortstop was Kevin Davis, a solid performer who had spent some time at Double-A the season before. Behind the plate were Mike Dotzler and Gilberto Roca. Both hit some big home runs while sharing the catching responsibilities.

Tony Chance was our left fielder and John Rigos patrolled center field as well as anyone in the league. Both could hit, and both were solid on defense. We also had a player from the Mexican League, Matias Carrillo, a designated hitter who sometimes played first base as well as the outfield.

*Tony Chance getting ready to hit during the 1987 season. He finished the season with a .318 average, 23 HR's, and 96 RBI's.*

Our pitching staff was anchored by Bill Copp, Bill Sampen, Jose Melendez, Orlando Lind, and the Pirates' second round draft pick from the year before, Mike Walker.

During the month of May, my wife, who was expecting our second child, decided to stop working at the ballpark while we awaited the arrival. She had been in charge of our souvenir operation. During her absence we learned to appreciate the job she did, as we had a difficult time finding a replacement that could handle her duties as efficiently.

Although she was no longer working, she continued coming to the park. When she realized we were having problems covering for her, she decided to return to work even though the baby was due any day. On May 12th, shortly after arriving home from the ballpark after our game, Sue began experiencing labor pains. We spent most of the night at the hospital before the doctor finally decided it was a false alarm.

We were less than halfway through a seven game homestand. I wouldn't let Sue work the following night, even though she wanted to. The next day she seemed fine, so I gave in and she returned. We left the ballpark around midnight and went home to bed. Sue woke me shortly before 5 a.m. and told me that it was time to go to the hospital again. This time it was for real, and our son Justen was born at 6:41 that morning.

After leaving the hospital a little while later, I went home and showered, then headed back to the park to prepare for the game that night. We were expecting our largest crowd of the season, and we weren't disappointed. Just further evidence that the show must go on!

As the first half of the season was winding down, the Pirates made a trade with the New York Mets, sending Bill Almon to New York for Al Pedrique and Scott Little. Little had been playing for the Lynchburg Mets and was assigned to Salem. Outfielder Jeff Cook, who had been struggling at Double-A, was also sent to us.

Our club had started off slowly, but when we beat Winston-Salem on the final day of the first half, we jumped over two teams, moving from last to second as the half closed. This was an omen of things to come. Our bullpen had been shaky in the first half, but veteran Clyde Reichard was signed as a free agent right after the half ended, and Paul Wilmet was assigned to us in July. We were poised to make a move as the second half got into high gear.

Demeter began working Little out at third base to try to get him into the line-up every day. The addition of Jeff Cook in the outfield with Rigos and Chance made us even stronger. Cook was also a tremendous base stealer, adding another dimension to our offense.

We started the second half with four straight losses but then reeled off fourteen victories in our next seventeen games, including eight in a row, to climb to the top of our division. In the month of July, the club posted a record of 22-6 while no other club in the league played above .500. We opened up a sizeable lead.

Because our ballpark is located in a residential neighbor-hood, we sometimes have to deal with problems that most ballparks don't have. Just beyond our short right field wall are a row of houses. Over the years many windows and doors have been damaged and broken by balls leaving our park during batting practice and games. To keep our neighbors happy, we've always paid for the damages.

During the season, a window was knocked out right before a ballgame, and the homeowner came into the office with a bill. We realized that he had made the repairs himself but had added a labor charge of $60. I offered to pay him for the replacement of the window but refused to pay what we felt was an exorbi-tant amount for labor. He stormed out of the office with his bill in his hand.

A short while later, as the gates were open and fans were arriving for our game that evening, our irate neighbor showed up with his new window. He walked through an open gate leading to an access road in the right-field corner of the sta-dium. He stood in the access road and began shouting obsceni-ties at me, smashed his new window in that access road, then stormed out of the ballpark. It didn't solve his problem but apparently made him feel better. We never heard from him again.

Shortly after the midway point of the season, I went into the park just before we were to open the gates for a game. At least a half dozen employees, including our public address announcer, Jeff Dickerson, were congregated in the outfield. They were pointing at something nearby and started running toward it. Upon closer inspection, it appeared to be a large rat.

They chased it from left center field toward the left field corner. Suddenly, the rat reached the wall and stopped. What's that old saying about never cornering a rat? Well, they had the opportunity to see why. The rat turned and started toward the group of employees. They began to run in the other direction with the rat in pursuit.

As the group retreated to center field, the rat stopped. The group then regained its courage and started chasing the rat again. Once more, the rat stopped at the wall and turned and began chasing the employees. It looked like a scene from Mack Sennett's Keystone Kop capers, with the employees chasing the rat, then the rat chasing them, and so on. It finally ended when Dickerson fired a golf ball at the rat, missing the rat but hitting the outfield wall and ricocheting back, striking the rat on the rebound and killing it.

The Carolina League All-Star game was held at the Peninsula ballpark in Hampton, Virginia., in mid-July. We placed five players on the Northern Division squad: outfielders Chance and Rigos, shortstop Davis, second baseman Moser, and pitcher Bill Copp. Steve Demeter served as a coach because of our second-place finish in the first half.

The host club is responsible for lining up the hotel for the event, along with a banquet to honor the players selected to participate. Traditionally, all of the league executives get together during this event and a league meeting is held.

For some unexplained reason, the Peninsula club lined up a motel without enough rooms to accommodate everyone. Some of the front office people from around the league were unable to get into the main motel. The property did contain several storage and maintenance buildings, and they tried unsuccessfully to convince some of the people who couldn't be accommodated to stay in these maintenance sheds.

A league meeting was scheduled for the afternoon we arrived, and problem number two developed when no one could find the meeting room. Upon checking with motel management, we were informed that the property contained no meeting rooms. They did offer to set up about twenty chairs in a large guest room, and all the league executives squeezed in for the meeting. Whether it was due to a lack of air conditioning or just the combination of the mid-July heat and too many people occupying too little space, it was more than a little uncomfortable during that meeting.

It became even more uncomfortable for the Peninsula general manager when someone raised the question about what time the bus would arrive the next day to bring the players to the ballpark for the game. As soon as the question was asked, all eyes turned to him. That classic look of "I knew there was something I forgot" appeared immediately on his face. He excused himself and said he would check on it right away!

The next major problem took place that night when the league banquet was held in the motel bar. The bar was large enough to accommodate thirty to forty people comfortably. We had more than forty players alone, along with the entire league front office personnel, league directors, media members, and some family members of players and league executives — more than double the room's capacity.

More than half the people in attendance were positioned at tables outside the building on the grassy lawn. Fortunately, the weather was outstanding, but this setting was not conducive to our accustomed banquet and awards ceremony. In addition, the bar was open to the public and people just drifted into the already-overcrowded room, not realizing what was going on. Because of this debacle, the league instituted a rule requiring league president John Hopkins to oversee all future All-Star game plans to prevent a recurrence.

On the field the next day, the Northern Division All-Stars lost to the South, 4-1. Our club, however, certainly deserved to be well represented, as several players had achieved recognition for their play during the first half.

John Rigos was named the Pittsburgh Pirates minor league player of the month for April; he posted a .378 average, along with 15 runs scored, seven driven in, and eight stolen bases during the month. Tony Chance was the Carolina League player of the month of May with a .357 average, eight home runs, 25 RBI; he also shared the Pirates' minor league player of the month award for May with teammate pitcher Bill Copp. Copp posted a 5-1 record in May.

Our club made it three months in a row when Jeff King received the Pirates minor league player of the month award for June, along with Jose Lind of the Triple-A Vancouver club. King hit .310 with ten homers and 29 RBI in June.

At the midway point of the season, our club had hit 79 home runs, and we were on a franchise record-setting attendance pace, having attracted more than 52,000 fans.

As the month of July came to a close, our torrid pace put us nine games in front with a month left to play. On August 21, a crowd of 3,674 pushed our season attendance total to 106,103, surpassing the all-time franchise record of 102,456 set in 1980. Then, on Sunday afternoon August 23rd, we beat Peninsula on the road while Prince William lost that evening at Lynchburg, clinching the second half title for our club. Salem would be hosting its first play-off game since 1972.

Hagerstown had won the first half in the Northern Division and had the option to host game one or games two and three in the best-of-three opening rounds. They elected to open the series in Salem, then return home for game two, and if necessary, game three.

Winston-Salem had won the first half in the Southern Division, and they decided to open their series on the road as well, taking on second-half winner Kinston.

The atmosphere at Municipal Field was electric on that evening of August 31st as the play-offs got underway. It had been 15 years since Municipal Field had hosted a play-off game, and only a handful of those in attendance could remember that last encounter.

The game started nearly an hour late due to two heavy but brief rain showers. After pulling the tarp off the field the second time, the grounds crew, myself included, was able to get the field ready for play.

The Suns went down in the top of the first inning and the hungry Salem crowd came to life as the Bucs came to bat. With one out, Steve Moser and John Rigos collected back-to-back singles, then Tony Chance walked to load the bases. Hagerstown pitcher Rob Walton then struck out Matias Carrillo for out number two. This brought Scott Little to the plate. The crowd exploded as he lined a change-up over the top of the scoreboard in left center field. The Bucs were up 4-0.

The teams traded runs in the fifth to make it a 5-1 contest. The Suns then got to Bucs ace Mike Walker with two runs in the sixth before Clyde Reichard put out the fire. The score now stood at 5-3.

Demeter brought in ace stopper Paul Wilmet to start the eighth inning. After a walk and a strikeout to open the frame, he was touched for a double off the fence, putting runners on second and third with only one out. The next batter hit a shot up the middle that Wilmet flagged down. He fired a strike to catcher Mike Dotzler as the runner on third tried to score. There was a violent collision at the plate, but Dotzler came up holding the ball and the runner was out.

The next hitter bounced weakly back to the mound, and Wilmet threw him out to end the inning. He then retired the side in order in the ninth to preserve the victory.

Game two was scheduled in Hagerstown the next night. Back-to-back triples by Moser and Rigos, followed by a walk to Chance and a three-run homer by Little, hit into a very stiff wind, enabled us to erase a 1-0 second inning deficit and take the lead, 4-1 in the top of the third.

The Suns came right back with three in the bottom of the inning to tie the game at 4-4. Clyde Reichard pitched out of a difficult situation in the fifth after coming on in relief of starter Orlando Lind, but the Suns managed to push across the lead run. It was all they would get off Reichard.

An RBI double by Scott Little in the seventh tied the score at 5. The score remained deadlocked until the top of the ninth, when Steve Moser doubled to left-center with one out. He took third when John Rigos grounded out to first for out number two. This brought up Tony Chance, who had led the team during the regular season with 96 RBI. After foul tipping a 2-2 pitch, the right-hand hitting Chance drove the next pitch the opposite way, over the first baseman's head into right field to score Moser with the go-ahead run.

For the second consecutive night, Paul Wilmet retired the side in the ninth inning to pick up the save. Reichard picked up the win, and our team had won the Northern Division title.

In the Southern Division, Kinston had beaten Winston-Salem in game one, but we didn't yet know the final score from their second game. We knew we were hosting games one and two in the best-of-five championship series but we didn't know when. If Kinston won, game one would take place the very next night. If Winston-Salem won, the two teams would meet in a deciding third game the following night, and we would get a night off. They were in extra innings when we left the ballpark in Hagerstown.

The ballclub stayed over in Hagerstown that night, but Jon Kaufman and I headed back down the highway to Salem to begin preparation for our next game, considering that it might be the next night. After our four-hour drive from Hagerstown, we immediately went to the office, called the Howe News Bureau, and were informed that Kinston had beaten Winston-Salem, 10-7 in 12 innings. We would be hosting the Indians in less than 24 hours.

We had beaten Kinston the last six times we played them during the regular season, but they had scored 21 runs in their two-game sweep over Winston-Salem. Obviously, they were hitting the ball well. Game one would pit Bill Sampen against Kinston's Mike Walker (both teams had a pitcher named Mike Walker).

Sampen hurled seven outstanding scoreless innings to cool off the hot Indian bats. He allowed just four singles and a pair of walks while striking out nine.

In the meantime the Bucs kept chipping away at Walker, starting with Jeff Cook's lead-off double in the bottom of the first. He took third on a wild pitch, then scored when Indian's catcher Tom Lampkin's throw went into left field. In the third, Kevin Davis doubled, then later scored on a sacrifice fly by Steve Moser. In the sixth, Scott Little singled to center, then Matias Carrillo homered to give the Bucs a 4-0 lead.

Kevin Davis led off the seventh with a double and came around to score run number five on a double by Moser. Scott Ruskin singled in the eighth in front of Mike Dotzler's RBI double to make it 6-0.

Paul Wilmet was called on once more to shut the door. He finally proved to be human when he yielded a two-run homer in the ninth inning to Joey (Albert) Belle. Belle had just been signed by the Indians out of LSU a week earlier. The runs were the first allowed by Wilmet in 14 2/3 innings, but not enough for the Indians. The final score was 6-2.

Game two was scheduled for the following night, and our starting pitching was beginning to run a little thin. Two of our starters, Jose Melendez and Martin Hernandez, were both complaining of sore arms. The Pirates had sent us Mike York, a pitcher from Macon, the Pirate affiliate directly below us. York had posted 17 wins at Macon but had yet to pitch for Salem. We had no idea what to expect.

York was magnificent. He hurled 6 ⅔ scoreless innings, giving up just three hits and allowing no runner past second base. He struck out eight.

Kinston starter Kevin Wickander kept the Bucs' hitters off balance early in the game, not allowing a hit for four innings. The Bucs did manage to push across a run in the fourth on three walks and a wild pitch, to take the lead.

Scott Ruskin homered in the fifth for the Bucs' second run. In the sixth, John Rigos doubled and Tony Chance homered to make it 4-0. The Bucs then broke the game open with three in the bottom of the seventh on RBI singles by Cook and Moser, and a John Rigos sacrifice fly.

The Indians did manage a run in the eighth off Clyde Reichard, but the Bucs had a commanding 2-0 lead in the best-of-five series by virtue of this 7-1 win. The remaining games would be played at Grainger Stadium in Kinston.

The Bucs had now beaten the Indians eight consecutive times. The club was not concerned about having to win a game on the road, either, having posted a road record of 26-9 in the second half, along with an additional road win at Hagerstown to wrap up the Northern Division play-offs. The pressure was definitely on Kinston.

Steve Demeter was planning on using his ace starter, our Mike Walker, to try to close out the series. Walker would be pitching with only three days' rest. Right before leaving the hotel for the game, Demeter received a call from the Pirates telling him they had decided that he should not use Walker on only three days' rest.

Demeter then decided to go with right-hander Rob Hatfield. Hatfield had started only twice all season. He pitched well, but the defense was a little shaky behind him and he left in the sixth inning, trailing 4-0. Mark Gilles held Salem hitless until the sixth inning, and kept the Bucs off the board until the eighth, when they finally broke through for a pair of runs on Scott Ruskin's RBI double and a run-scoring infield hit by Kevin Davis.

The Bucs threatened again in the ninth off reliever Mike Farr, when Tony Chance walked with one out and the red-hot Scott Little lined a shot to right field. Indians' right fielder Jim Bruske made a great catch and doubled Chance off first to end the game. The series now stood at two games to one.

Game four would take place the following night, on Saturday, September 5, 1987. This time our Mike Walker was ready to pitch. It rained for much of the day in Kinston, but the Indians' grounds crew was able to get the field ready by game time. Because it was Saturday, a large contingent of Salem fans was able to make the trip, and they were loudly cheering on their Buccaneers.

An even larger contingent of Salem faithful were sitting at home listening to their radios to hear if the Bucs could bring home the first Salem championship in 13 years. One of my goals when taking over the day-to-day operation of the club had been to get our games on the radio. In all of the years of pro baseball in Salem, the club had never had more than a handful of games broadcast. We had finally succeeded in lining up a station, WTOY, and all 140 regular season games, as well as the play-offs, were being broadcast for the first time ever. We were extremely pleased with our first-year broadcast team of Brian Barnhart and Dan Bonner.

Brian Barnhart was just 22 years old, and it was his first season as a full-time baseball play-by-play broadcaster. The Illinois native had graduated from college just a year earlier. He handled all 140 regular season games as well as the play-offs.

Dan Bonner worked with Brian during all home games and also helped out occasionally on the road. At the time, Bonner lived in Roanoke and was already making a name for himself during the winter months as a college basketball analyst for ESPN, Raycom Sports, and Jefferson-Pilot Teleproductions.

Barnhart was broadcasting live back to the Roanoke Valley as Mike Walker and his teammates attempted to bring home the title. Walker had been outstanding all season long, but especially during the second half, when he posted a 7-0 record on the road with a 1.53 ERA.

Walker was overpowering, relying primarily on his fastball and occasionally mixing in a good breaking pitch. He allowed only two singles through eight innings and did not allow a runner to reach second base until the eighth.

Tony Ghelfi was pitching well for Kinston, but the Bucs were able to get to him for a pair of runs in the third on RBI singles by Little and Carrillo with two out.

A strange situation occurred with the Indians batting in the bottom of the seventh and two out. Jim Bruske hit a bullet that nearly decapitated a sprawling Mike Walker, who ducked under the line drive that went through the box and into center field for an apparent base hit.

As Bruske stood at first base, Bucs catcher Mike Dotzler retrieved Bruske's bat and handed it to home plate umpire B.B. Guttieriez. Dotzler had spotted something the night before but waited until Bruske got a hit to bring it to the umpire's attention. Guttieriez inspected the bat, then called Kinston manager Mike Hargrove in from the third base coaching box to present the evidence. He then called Bruske out and also tossed him out of the game for using an illegally grooved bat. The inning was over.

As the game moved into the top of the eighth, the Bucs exploded. Scott Little led off with a double, then scored on a base hit by Carrillo. Tony Chance followed with a single, moving Carrillo to third and taking second when the throw went into third, unsuccessfully trying to nab Carrillo.

Hargrove then went to his bullpen, bringing in Charles Soos to pitch to Scott Ruskin. Ruskin doubled to right, knocking in both Carrillo and Chance and giving the Bucs a 5-0 lead.

Walker breezed through the eighth, allowing only one hitter to reach first base on an error. He opened the ninth by striking out the first batter on three pitches. The Bucs were just two outs away from the championship, but Walker appeared to run out of gas. He walked the next batter, before giving up back-to-back singles to yield his first run, leaving runners on the corners.

Demeter went to the mound and made the move to bring in Paul Wilmet. Wilmet induced Albert Belle to hit a bouncer to short, where the usually sure-handed Kevin Davis booted the ball. A run scored on the play, making it 5-2, with runners on first and second and the tying run at the plate. Wilmet persuaded Lampkin to ground into a force at second for out number two. He then went to a 2-2 count on Kerry Richardson before breaking off a wicked fork ball that Richardson swung at and missed, bringing the '87 Carolina League season to a close.

The Buccaneers were the champions. It was a great feeling being down on that field with a super bunch of guys who had pulled together and battled back all season. It was a storybook finish in a season of firsts — our first season back with the Pirates, our first season with all of our games on the radio, and our first play-off game in 15 years. And now, finally, we were bringing our first championship in 13 years back to the Roanoke Valley (Salem had won the league title in 1974, but with a single division format, a play-off was not necessary because Salem won both halves).

This was a good club, as evidenced by the fact that they posted the best overall record in the league (85-60 including play-offs). In addition, the club led the league in team batting (.278), runs scored (771), hits (1,328), home runs (149, a new franchise record), stolen bases (218), team ERA (3.80), and shut outs (10). They finished second in the league in saves (40).

Mike Walker posted a 12-5 record. Paul Wilmet saved 17 games, including the three in the play-offs. Tony Chance finished third in the league in hitting with a .318 average, along with 23 home runs and 96 RBI. Jeff King finished second in the league in home runs with 26, trailing only Prince William's Hensley Meulen's 28, despite having been promoted to Double-A Harrisburg around the end of July.

Individual honors went to Tony Chance and John Rigos; both were named to the year-end Carolina League All-Star team. We felt Steve Demeter should have been Manager of the Year but the award went to Mike Hargrove. The league Most

*Bringing home the hardware . . . Mills Cup, Carolina League Championship trophy, on its way to Salem following final play-off game in Kinston, September 1987.*

Valuable Player was Kinston third baseman Casey Webster, but we thought Tony Chance was more deserving.

However, Kelvin summed it up best in the visitors' clubhouse in Kinston after we'd wrapped up the title. He said, "They may have gotten all of the individual awards, but we got this one!" as he held up the league championship trophy.

Indeed, the Bucs were back!

*The debonair "Clown Prince of Baseball," Max Patkin, at Municipal Field in 1987.*

# 8 What Do We Do For An Encore?

It felt great to win the championship in 1987. In fact, it was one of those rare occasions when you wish it could go on forever. Such is not reality, however, and after a few weeks of basking in the glory and savoring the great feeling of satisfaction, it was time to move on.

We knew it would be nearly impossible to top the '87 season, but we were already hearing talk that our '88 club might be even more talented. The Pirate affiliate directly below us, Macon, was solid all season and had some very good prospects. The club below Macon, Watertown, in the New York-Penn League, won its division title before losing in the play-offs to Geneva. Our club would consist primarily of players from these two teams.

The club directly above us, Harrisburg, of the Double-A Eastern League, also won its league championship. Indeed, things were looking good for the future of the Pittsburgh Pirates.

The big league club had improved from its last place finish in 1986 to a competitive 80-82 record, nearly cracking the .500 mark for the first time since 1983. They had jumped two spots to finish in fourth place under second year manager Jim Leyland.

Some changes had taken place in the organization following the season. The Macon club in the South Atlantic League moved to Augusta, Georgia, and the Triple-A affiliation in Vancouver of the Pacific Coast League was moved to Buffalo of the American Association.

We also were making changes in Salem. Kelvin was dissatisfied with the way some of the day-to-day duties assigned to Jon Kaufman were being handled. Jon had done very well in sales, but during the season his primary responsibility was running our concessions operation. Kelvin felt that we could make big improvements in that area and had talked to Jon in great detail about it following the '86 season.

As the '87 season came to a close, Kelvin decided that Jon had not shown the kind of improvement he expected and it was time to make a change. I felt bad for Jon, having worked side by side with him for two seasons, but Kelvin owned the club and it ultimately was his decision. We immediately began a search for Jon's replacement.

As we moved into November, we entered into an agreement with a different radio station to carry all of our games during the upcoming season. We were moving from WTOY, the first station willing to carry all 140 live broadcasts, to WROV, one of the more established and well-known Roanoke Valley radio stations. It's amazing how the successful past season, both on the field and on the air, was opening new doors for us.

Unlike in the majors, where radio and TV stations are willing to pay a team for its broadcast rights, in the minors, especially the lower minors, it is quite different. In essence, we purchase the airtime from the radio station, paying an agreed-upon fee to get our games on the air. We retain advertising rights, enabling us to sell the advertising with the hope of at least covering our expenses, which include, in addition to the fee paid to the radio station, the salary, transportation, meal money, and overnight expenses of the announcer or announcers, and all telephone line charges and installation fees for the broadcasts. Radio is not a big money maker for most clubs, but many feel that as long as they aren't losing a bundle, it provides a three-hour forum on a daily basis to promote the club. Not all clubs have this same arrangement, but most are similar.

One of the major reasons we changed radio stations, in addition to moving over to a much more established station, was the fact that WTOY was authorized to broadcast only until sundown. This meant that there were times during our inaugural broadcast season when we were forced to sign off the air before the conclusion of the game.

We got around this problem as well as possible by working out an arrangement with the two largest local cable TV companies to broadcast the audio feed of all our games over one of their message channels. Our broadcaster, Brian Barnhart, would start directing listeners to tune into their local cable TV outlet on nights when we were approaching time for our station to sign off the air.

It wasn't the greatest arrangement in the world, but it enabled us to get all of our games on the air. Our new contract with WROV would resolve that problem once and for all, as its license enabled the station to broadcast 24 hours a day.

No sooner had we resolved this problem than our next radio problem arose. Barnhart was hired by the Triple-A Oklahoma City 89ers. We had lost our outstanding young play-by-play man. We knew Brian was good but we'd been hoping to keep him for at least one more season. Just like the minor league players, the majority of minor league broadcasters and front-office personnel are trying to work their way up the ladder to the major leagues as well.

In just a couple of weeks, our front office staff of three had dwindled to myself. We now had to find another announcer as well as a replacement for Jon Kaufman.

Our search for a replacement for Kaufman was not going well. We were looking for the right combination of work ethic and experience and, when we found this combination, we were having no luck at prying these people away from their current situations.

One of the first people we tried to persuade was Marty Nash. Marty was coming off a very successful second year at the helm of the Burlington Indians. They had led the Appalachian League in attendance, and Marty had been named the Appy League Executive of the Year. He was happy working for Miles Wolff and, although we offered him more money than he was currently making, he was content to remain in Burlington.

Fortunately, my search for a new play-by-play man was going much better. Without even advertising the opening, tapes and resumes were streaming in. Such is the nature of the baseball play-by-play business. It's amazing how many people in this country would give anything to become baseball broadcasters.

After screening dozens of tapes and resumes, we offered the position to Dave Newman. Dave was more than adequate on the air, but additionally possessed a great deal of sales experience. He spent the 1987 season as the back-up play-by-play announcer for the Lynchburg Mets, the same position Brian Barnhart held in '86 before we hired him.

We were certainly pleased with Brian so we decided to take that same route again by hiring Dave. Brian may have been slightly better on the air, but Dave was much more polished in the other important aspects of the business, especially sales.

Speaking of Lynchburg, following the 1987 season the New York Mets ended one of the most successful runs in minor league history by severing ties with Lynchburg. The move followed a current trend when the Mets placed their advanced "A" operation in the Florida State League to utilize their new spring training complex at Port St. Lucie.

Dwight Gooden, Darryl Strawberry, and Lenny Dykstra were just a few of the many stars to pass through Lynchburg on their way to the major leagues. Starting with the second half of the 1982 season, Lynchburg had finished in first place for an unprecedented seven consecutive halves.

The '83 Lynchburg squad captured the league title while posting the best record in pro baseball at 99-43, led by Dykstra's .358 average and a league-record 105 stolen bases. Gooden had a 19-4 record, but suffered his first Shea Stadium loss that season at the hands of Salem, when the two clubs played a Carolina League game in Shea as part of a pre-game promotion for the New York Mets.

During the '87 season, Gooden was sent back to Lynchburg on a one-game rehabilitation assignment and City Stadium was jammed beyond capacity for his return. With the loss of the Mets, the Boston Red Sox went into Lynchburg.

Also during the fall, we received a call from a movie production company that had set up shop in Durham, North Carolina. Work was beginning on a movie about minor league baseball. The producers wanted permission to use our uniforms. After receiving a number of assurances that the uniforms would be returned in the same condition in which they were sent, we agreed to allow their use in the movie.

We had no idea whether the movie would be successful, but the bulk of it was being shot at Durham Athletic Park, home of the Bulls. The Bulls are also a member of the Carolina League, and we were able to check out the movie people by placing a call to the Durham club. We were informed that Miles Wolff was serving as an advisor to the producers.

A number of other clubs in both the Carolina and South Atlantic Leagues also were contacted with regard to use of their uniforms. Active and former players living nearby were hired to handle bit parts in the film as well, including one of our pitchers, Tim Kirk. Tim lived in Chapel Hill, North Carolina, and he ended up appearing in several scenes.

The movie was scheduled to be released sometime in late spring or early summer. Kevin Costner and Susan Sarandon were the stars, and the "Clown Prince of Baseball", Max Patkin, also was scheduled to appear. The name of the movie was "Bull Durham".

We spent a great deal of time interviewing candidates for the position of assistant GM at the baseball Winter Meetings in Dallas in early December. Kelvin had decided that I should assume the title of general manager instead of director of baseball operations, as it would be less confusing as to who was running the club on a day-to-day basis.

We hired Jim Tessmer to fill the position as my assistant. He had worked for the Pawtucket Red Sox of the Triple-A International League in 1984 before moving to the New York Yankees' front office until February 1986. He left the Yankees to join the Watertown Pirates for the '86 season, then in '87 was hired as the business manager of the Macon Pirates in the South Atlantic League. He was familiar with the Pirates' organization and had some solid experience. He had also worked briefly for Dennis Bastien in Charleston, West Virginia, in early 1987 prior to Macon.

Dennis owned the Winston-Salem club in our league as well as the Martinsville club in the Appalachian League. At the end of the '86 season, he landed an expansion team in the South Atlantic League in Charleston and was trying to find someone to operate the club for him while he continued to operate in Winston-Salem. He called to see if I'd be interested.

I've always liked Dennis personally and feel that he and his wife Lisa did an outstanding job running first-class baseball operations. But things were beginning to come together nicely in Salem and we were just scratching the surface, as far as reaching our potential. I was not interested in leaving the job I had just started in Salem.

Fortunately, it never got to the point where we officially discussed the Charleston position. He called me to feel me out, and I told him that I really didn't think I was ready to leave Salem. He said that, before he made me an offer, he would call Kelvin to get his permission to talk with me, as this is standard procedure in pro baseball when approaching someone already employed by another organization. I never did hear from him again regarding Charleston, so I assume he did not get permission from Kelvin. It was all just as well.

While in Dallas, we also hired an administrative assistant named Torree Selders. She was a native of Oklahoma and had worked for the Oklahoma City 89ers the year before.

Murray Cook rejoined the club on a full-time basis as the director of stadium operations. He had worked for us as an advisor on stadium and groundskeeping operations for the past two years. He had served as the head groundskeeper for the Salem club throughout the late 1970s and early 1980s before moving on to Double-A Charlotte of the Southern League, then to Salt Lake City of the Triple-A Pacific Coast League, before leaving the game. Cook had returned to his hometown of Salem and was interested in getting back into baseball full-time.

As we approached the new year, our front office staff had expanded to five full-time employees, the largest year-round staff in Salem baseball history.

In mid-December, the Pittsburgh Pirates named Jay Ward our field manager for the upcoming season. Ward had spent the previous season as the major league hitting instructor for the New York Yankees. In 1986 he managed the Cincinnati Reds Double-A Vermont team to the Eastern League championship.

Ward had begun his managerial career in the Minnesota Twins organization in 1972, then got out of the game for ten years before returning with the Phillies organization in '83 at Bend, Oregon, in the Northwest League. He was promoted by the Phillies to Spartanburg in the South Atlantic League in '84, before moving to the Reds organization with Cedar Rapids in the Midwest League in '85.

Ward played professionally for 15 years as an infielder and outfielder, reaching the major leagues briefly with the Twins in '63 and '64, and with the Reds in 1970.

On January 22nd, we flew Ward into Salem to meet with the local media. I escorted him around the Roanoke Valley for most of the day, and we hit it off. We were impressed with him and felt that the upcoming season would be a good one in terms of the cooperation we could expect from our manager. How wrong we were!

While he was in Salem, we showed Ward the clubhouse facilities. He was impressed, but made a number of suggestions on things that he would like to see done prior to his arrival from spring training. We told him we'd see what we could do, but really didn't expect to be able to accomplish most of the things requested. He was practically looking for us to redesign the clubhouse after the city had spent a large sum to upgrade the facility only a year earlier.

When Ward arrived from spring training and found his requests had not been met, he was upset, to say the least. From that point on, our relationship was stormy. We weren't the only people in the league who had a stormy relationship with him. As the season progressed, we received a number of complaints from the other clubs in the league with regard to his attitude and lack of cooperation.

We received even more complaints regarding our trainer, Bruce Klein. Klein served as Ward's go-between with the front office, and he constantly came to us with a list of demands. Never did he simply request anything. It was always a demand. Between the two of them, things were very uncomfortable for our front office.

*Bucs' Manager Jay Ward studies the hitter from behind the batting cage.*

Ward was an excellent field manager with a talented club. Despite being no-hit during the opening week, we started the season playing well and built up a sizable lead in our division, capped by an eight-game winning streak in late May to virtually assure us of winning our second consecutive half.

Ward was a workhorse, and he expected nothing but the best from his players. He was able to push them to their limits and get the most out of their talents. This ability definitely would become an asset as the season progressed, as time and again Ward had to rebuild practically from scratch because the Pirates kept inflicting player moves upon us. We had 66 separate player transactions that season.

The team remained virtually intact during the early days of the season. That eight-game winning streak was part of a tear that saw the team post 24 victories in 31 games, clinching the first-half Northern Division crown on June 14th in Kinston. We were assured of our second straight play-off appearance.

That also was the start of the mass player exodus. The day after clinching the half, two of our best players were promoted to Double-A Harrisburg. Infielder Kevin Burdick had been leading the Carolina League with 49 RBI, including 25 in his last 14 games. He was hitting .321 with 9 home runs.

We also lost pitcher Rick Reed. Reed was our most consistent starter, posting a 6-2 record after being converted from the bullpen on May 7th. He compiled an ERA of 1.37, and his two losses were by scores of 2-1 and 2-0. He became a rags-to-riches story during the season. After a horrible spring and getting hammered out of the bullpen early in the year, he got a spot start when an injury created an opening in our rotation.

After going to Harrisburg from Salem, Reed made two starts, posting a 1-0 record. He hurled 16 innings, allowing just two earned runs while striking out 17. From there, he was called up to Triple-A Buffalo, where he started nine games, tossed two shutouts and won five of seven decisions, with a 1.64 ERA.

His next stop was Pittsburgh, where, on August 8th, he made his major league debut against the New York Mets, working eight scoreless innings, allowing just three hits, and picking up a 1-0 victory. Not bad for a guy who started the season as a shaky reliever on the Class A level.

Earlier in the half season we lost our starting shortstop, Tom Shields. Shields was hitting .314 with three homers, 25 RBI, and ten stolen bases in just 45 games before being promoted to Harrisburg. Burdick started the season playing second base, but moved over to short when Shields was promoted.

We also lost Scott Ruskin, who started the season as our first baseman, as well as pitcher Mike York. York went 9-2 in 13 starts, posting a 2.68 ERA. Indeed, our level of talent may have been better than that of our '87 club, but the problem we had was holding on to it long enough to see if any type of competitive team would evolve in the second half.

The night before we clinched the first half title on the road in Kinston, a local movie theater in Salem was hosting a private screening of the movie "Bull Durham". We had promoted the event for several weeks at our park by giving away free passes for the screening via lucky number drawings during our games.

We also hosted a "Bull Durham" night, giving away Kevin Costner posters, "Bull Durham" baseball cards, tote bags, and even some steaks when a home run was hit during the game that night, just like in a scene from the movie itself.

With our club on the road, our entire front office was able to attend the private screening. We had no idea what we were about to see, and the first impressions were mixed as the movie ended. We received a wide variety of feedback from the other viewers. Most liked it, but many were appalled by the language and amount of sexual innuendo, not to mention some of the more blatant sex scenes.

From a positive standpoint, people were talking about it. The film immediately took off at the box office. It created a new interest in minor league baseball and we definitely were a beneficiary. Even today, we hear comments about that movie and the name Durham Bulls has become almost mythical. The Bulls were successful even before the movie, but since then have grown tremendously.

Success breeds imitation, especially in the movies, and shortly after "Bull Durham" became a huge hit, several more baseball movies were released, including "Field of Dreams", "Major League", and "Eight Men Out". These movies further contributed to the increasing popularity of pro baseball.

Despite this new found popularity as a result of the movie, we were continuing to run into problems on the field. We lost several more players shortly after winning the first half title, including pitcher Bill Sampen and outfielder Tony Longmire. Longmire was leading our team and was among the league leaders with 11 home runs and 40 RBI, at the time of his promotion.

Also, one of our players suffered a serious concussion one night during a game in Durham. Scott Henion, a relief pitcher, was hit in the forehead by a line drive off the bat of Theron Todd, and was knocked unconscious. The ball hit him so hard that it bounded all the way into the dugout for a ground rule double. There was a great deal of concern during what seemed like an eternity, as both team trainers and then a doctor who had been called out of the stands tended to Scott. He lay motionless on the field for a lengthy period of time before being removed on a stretcher and rushed to a local hospital. He was out of action for some time, but fortunately was able to return to the active roster before the end of the season.

We were also experiencing other problems on the field, most stemming from the fact that we seemed to be playing in a number of games involving beanballs. Several of our pitchers confided that they had been instructed at times to throw at opposing hitters. This led to at least a half-dozen bench clearing brawls. Our team had gotten a reputation, and it wasn't a good one. We spent most of our time at league meetings apologizing for the behavior of our club.

What should have been a fun season, already highlighted by a guaranteed berth in the play-offs for the second straight year, was not much fun at all. In addition to all of the player moves and problems on the field, our trainer had learned a new trick. He would run to the clubhouse repeatedly during games and call the pressbox to have me paged.

I was constantly being interrupted from my nightly duties by having to go to the pressbox to answer the phone. Bruce would be on the other end, complaining that there were kids climbing on the dugout or some fan was bothering him by trying to talk to him during the game. Rarely, if ever, was his problem one of any significance.

Despite all of the player moves, we still had eight team members named to the Northern Division All-Star team. Jay Ward was the Northern Division manager by virtue of our first-place finish in the first half and Bruce Klein was the trainer. We placed pitchers Tim Kirk and Stan Belinda, catcher Andy Hall, first baseman Junior Vizcaino, and outfielders Julio Peguero and Wes Chamberlain on the team. Also named to the team were pitcher York and outfielder Longmire, but both already had been promoted to Harrisburg.

The North beat the South 2-1 in the game played at Grainger Stadium in Kinston on July 20th. Outstanding pitching dominated the contest, with Stan Belinda hurling two impressive innings. Belinda was overpowering, allowing no runs and striking out four. Tim Kirk worked the final two innings, allowing only an unearned run and gaining the save.

One incident that stood out during the season took place at Municipal Field. We were hosting Hagerstown and had fallen way behind early in the game. Due to some injuries and player moves, our pitching staff was tired and overworked. When Hagerstown opened up a big lead, Ward decided not to burn up any more of his pitchers. Instead, he brought in pitching coach Chris Lein to pitch.

This substitution would have been all right if Chris had been on our active roster. When the umpire pointed out that Chris wasn't an eligible player, Ward threatened to pull his team off the field, claiming he had no one else available. Hagerstown manager Mike Hart immediately protested the action, but the game was allowed to continue with Lein on the hill. The situation was embarrassing to Chris and the league, and Ward was hit with a hefty fine by league president John Hopkins for making a travesty of the game. The protest by Hagerstown was unnecessary as they pummeled us anyway.

Another thing that stands out regarding the '88 season is the Peninsula club. After the All-Star game debacle in 1987, you would think things could only get better over on Virginia's peninsula. Think again!

For starters, owner Gil Granger decided to change the name of the club. They looked for something more appropriate for the area and decided to tap into the huge Navy base nearby, along with the rich naval tradition in the area. They came up with the Virginia Generals. Apparently no one told them that the rank of general doesn't exist in the Navy.

The second big mistake Granger made was naming his daughter, Gilinda, as the new general manager. She had no baseball background and couldn't even read a baseball statistics sheet until after assuming the position. She had also spent time

*Things had a tendency to get a little rough
during the 1988 season.*

in prison on a drug charge, and her relationship with her employees and ballplayers was turbulent at best.

Things were so bad on the peninsula that *Baseball America*, the baseball news publication, went so far as to call it "the worst franchise in baseball" in their September 25th issue that year. The article describing the situation mentioned that the director of beer sales was a 340-pound recovering alcoholic. His assistant was working for the club in lieu of being sent to jail for stealing a fire hydrant.

The club had gone through four groundskeepers, and once had even started a game before realizing home plate had been put in backwards. They played a game one night with only 25 people in the stands; each one was introduced over the public address system.

Our Carolina League guidelines dictate that the home club should start the umpires with a minimum of 18 baseballs each night. Gilinda was aware of this rule and, during their first game of the season, she gave the umpires 18 baseballs. Most clubs go through an average of about three to four dozen balls per game, so eighteen is a conservative minimum. Depending on the weather and the amount of balls hit out of play or scuffed up, the total actually used varies. Regardless, the home club must see to it that enough balls are provided to keep the game going.

Several innings into the first game, one of the batboys came to Gilinda to tell her that they were nearly out of baseballs and would need more. She told the batboy that they had already received their 18 balls for the night and she wouldn't give them any more. They ultimately had to stop the game while the umpires pleaded with her for more baseballs. She eventually was persuaded to supply enough to finish the game.

My favorite Generals story relates to their player caps. Traditionally, the players on each club receive new team caps at the start of the second half of the season. Gilinda decided that she could sell the old caps as souvenirs, so she required each player to turn in his old cap before receiving a new one.

The players decided to get back at her by urinating in their caps before turning them in. Unfortunately for them, Gilinda got the last laugh. After the players performed their trick, she refused to make the exchange and the players had to play in their damp, smelly, old caps.

We were never able to mount a serious run at the second-half title because of all the player changes. Hagerstown and Lynchburg fought right down to the last day of the season before Lynchburg clinched the title, setting up a first round play-off meeting between us and the Lynchburg Red Sox. Salem and Lynchburg, located only 50 miles apart, have always been rivals. Having won the first half, we had the option of opening the series in Lynchburg, then coming home for games two and three, or opening at home, then playing games two and three at Lynchburg.

Jay Ward wanted to open at home, then play two on the road. His logic was that he wanted the series to be decided in a "real" ballpark. He was not fond of Municipal Field and its short porches. On the other hand, we wanted the opportunity to host two play-off games, feeling that, if for no other reason, our fans deserved it. After all, we had set a franchise attendance record for the second year in a row. Hosting two games instead of one also made sense from a business standpoint. We went with our decision.

Even though our team was only a shell of the team that had won the first half, they played extremely well. Game one in Lynchburg saw us take a 3-0 lead with a run in the first and two in the second, thanks to a pair of RBI by Wes Chamberlain on a double and single. Pitcher Pete Murphy hurled 7 2/3 strong innings before being touched for a two-run homer by Paul Devlin on a 0-2 pitch to make it a 3-2 game.

With two out in the bottom of the eighth, Scott Cooper singled. Jay Ward then went to his bullpen and brought in his ace stopper, Stan Belinda. Belinda walked Mickey Pina, then Bob Zupcic singled up the middle. Center fielder Julio Peguero had a good shot at nailing Cooper at the plate but had trouble getting the ball out of his glove, and the tying run scored. The game went into extra innings.

With two outs in the bottom of the tenth, Cooper walked, then Pina nubbed a seeing eye base hit between third and short, enabling Cooper to race into third. Steve Buckholz, who had come on to pitch the tenth inning for the Bucs, then uncorked a wild pitch, allowing Cooper to cross the plate with the game winner.

Game two was played the following night back in Salem. With our backs to the wall, Ward decided to start Keith Richardson. Richardson was the Pirates' second round draft choice in June and had appeared in only two previous games since being recently promoted to Salem. He had a combined 9-2 win-loss record with Watertown and Augusta, with a 0.87 ERA.

Richardson went the distance, allowing just three hits while striking out ten. We jumped out to a 2-0 lead in the first inning, thanks to two heroes from the '87 club, Steve Moser and John Rigos. Moser slid in hard to break up a double play, allowing the first run to score. Then Rigos bowled over catcher Bruce Devlin at the plate to score on Orlando Merced's double.

We put the game away with five more runs in the second, highlighted by RBI hits by Steve Carter, Carlos Garcia, and Peguero. Two of the three hits allowed by Richardson were a pair of solo homers by Mickey Pina. The final score was 10-2.

This set up a climactic game three in Salem the next night. For the first time all season, the Bucs were shut out at home, falling to the L-Sox by the score of 5-0. Dave Walters tossed the shutout for the Sox, who jumped out to a 2-0 lead in the first on a pair of unearned runs. Mickey Pina clouted a three-run homer in the third to close out the scoring. It was his third of the series. Our season had come to an end.

Kinston defeated Lynchburg in the play-off finals, three games to two, to capture their first Carolina League title since 1962. They did it with strong pitching, led by lefthanded relief ace Kevin Bearse, with ten wins and 22 saves. He also recorded 127 strike outs in just 103 innings, and a 1.31 ERA.

Bernie Williams of Prince William won the league batting title with a .338 average. Kent Mercker of Durham led the league with the lowest ERA of any starting pitcher at 2.68, to go with a record of 11-4. Winston-Salem's Phil Harrison was

*Prince William Manager Wally Moon*
*did not agree with the umpire's call.*

14-4, and teammate Shawn Boske went 12-7. Lynchburg's
Mickey Pina was named the Most Valuable Player in the
league, as he led in homers with 21 and RBI with 108. His
manager Dick Berardino was named Manager of the Year,
before being promoted to the Boston Red Sox coaching staff
the following season.

Winston-Salem pitcher Bill Kazmierczak became the first pitcher in league history to pitch two no-hitters in the same season. Shortly afterwards he was promoted to Double-A.

Following the mid-season release of the movie "Bull Durham", the Durham Bulls set a Class A season attendance record by drawing 271,650 to Durham Athletic Park. This record shattered their own all-time mark, set just the year before with 217,012. The previous best all-time Class A record had been set by Greensboro in 1981, with 260,040.

We ended up drawing 119,966, topping our regular season record from the year before by more than 8,000. Overall, it was a good year for the league and another good season for us.

In a year that had started out so optimistically, our club made a valiant run at a second straight Carolina League title, only to fall short. We saw some talented players pass through: Kevin Burdick, Tommy Shields, Tony Longmire, Scott Ruskin, Rick Reed, and Mike York were with us early, Wes Chamberlain, Steve Carter, Carlos Garcia, and Orlando Merced were with us later on, and Julio Peguero and Stan Belinda were with us all season.

Surprisingly, we did not place a single player on the end-of-season All-Star team. The only possible explanation, based on all the talent we had, was that so few stuck around for any length of time. More than anything else, our encore season had been one of transition.

# 9 Rockin' In The Rain!

The transition was not limited to the field. After the '88 season ended, our front office also went through another transition of its own.

Torree Selders left to pursue other interests, primarily the trainer of one of the other clubs in our league. Her involvement with Mike Folga had begun shortly after her arrival. Mike was the trainer of the local East Coast Hockey League franchise during the winter months, then in the spring was employed by the Chicago Cubs as trainer for the Winston-Salem Spirits. He and Torree started dating before the season started.

We were also somewhat disappointed by the job done by Jim Tessmer. He made some inroads in sales, but left much to be desired in overseeing and supervising the concession operation. I admit that we had staffing problems, but we all felt we weren't making the kind of progress needed in the concession area. His problems included too few staff on big nights and too many on slow nights. His concession staff also gave him little respect.

As the season was winding down, he appeared to have lost control over his troops. He does deserve credit for making a great pizza. We probably received more compliments on our pizza that year than ever before or since, including seasons when we worked with an outside pizza vendor.

His work ethic and attitude were good, but he was over-matched, handling a role that he really wasn't qualified for. Unfortunately, we weren't in a position to assign him other duties and keep him around, even though we would have liked to. We needed someone to take charge of the concession responsibilities during the season, in addition to handling sales during the off-season. We began looking for a person to handle these duties.

There is a tendency to overlook the diverse skills required to be successful in this kind of position, especially at the lower minor league level where a single person has many responsibilities. As we were finding out, finding a concession manager who could also sell was not easy.

Another difficult position to fill is that of groundskeeper. We had one of the best in Murray Cook, who also did surprisingly well as a salesperson during the off-season. But shortly after we lost Torree and let Tessmer go, Murray informed us that he had accepted a job with the Harrisburg Senators. We had now lost our groundskeeper as well.

Our five-person front office staff had dwindled to just two, myself and Dave Newman. We spent a great deal of time searching for new staff members over the next few months.

The front office of the Pittsburgh Pirates was also going through a transition. As the major league season was winding down, a power struggle had apparently developed in Pittsburgh, and the board of directors decided to relieve Syd Thrift of his duties. On October 4th, Larry Doughty was named to replace Thrift on an interim basis. On November 7th, Doughty was hired as Thrift's permanent replacement. Doughty had been hired just a year earlier as a special assistant to Thrift.

By the time we headed off to the Baseball Winter Meetings in Atlanta in early December, we were still trying to fill all three front-office openings. Much of my time was spent reviewing resumes and interviewing potential employees. It was not the way I had originally planned to spend my time in Atlanta, but you do whatever it takes to get the job done.

Sam Clark had worked as our assistant groundskeeper during the past season, and also had handled a number of duties inside the stadium. He had worked for the club in a number of capacities over the years, starting as a batboy as a youngster. He attended the Winter Meetings to try to find a job with another club.

Before leaving for Atlanta, I had approached him about our head groundskeepers position, but he wanted to test the waters and see what else might be available. We continued to work on him at the Winter Meetings, and having him there worked to our advantage. He was able to see the incredible number of people trying to break into baseball, with only a few low-paying positions available.

It was an eye-opening experience for him and many others. Before leaving Atlanta, he agreed to sit down with me after we returned to Salem and seriously listen to my offer. It was one of the bright spots of our employee search in Atlanta.

The only other bright spot along those lines was finding a replacement for Torree. We hired an entry-level young woman named Peg Shaughnessy as an administrative assistant. We had no luck at all in hiring an assistant general manager and left Atlanta still searching for the right person.

Several days after returning to Salem, the Pirates informed us that Rocky Bridges would be our field manager in '89. Rocky had been in Buffalo the previous season, piloting the Triple-A Bisons. He was a real character and was constantly being quoted by major sports publications, including *Sports Illustrated*, *The Sporting News*, *USA Today*, and *Baseball America*. After what we had just endured, we were really looking forward to working with Rocky.

One of Rocky's greatest claims to fame in baseball circles has been teaching young players how to chew tobacco in both cheeks simultaneously, as well as teaching them how to chew tobacco and drink beer at the same time.

Rocky was born in Refugio, Texas, but now resides in Coeur D'Alene, Idaho. He was a major league infielder for 11 seasons, breaking in with the Brooklyn Dodgers in '51. He spent most of his big league career with Cincinnati, although he also played for Washington, Detroit, Cleveland, St. Louis, and the Los Angeles Angels.

The '89 season would mark the 20th year Bridges would manage professionally in the twenty-five years since his first manager's job at San Jose in 1964. During the other five years, he was involved as a coach and an instructor. Prior to the '88 season at Buffalo, Bridges was the Pirates Triple-A manager in '87 as well, at Vancouver in the Pacific Coast League. He was named P.C.L. Manager of the Year in both '74 and '77.

Shortly after the Christmas holidays, Peg Shaughnessy moved to Salem to assume her new position. We also convinced Sam Clark to accept the head groundskeepers job, but we were still unable to find an assistant GM.

As January wound down, we decided to fill the opening by bringing in an additional entry-level person to train in sales, and hiring several experienced concession employees from the previous season to handle the concession duties.

Our entry-level salesperson started in early February and it didn't take long to realize we had made a mistake. He got upset whenever our Friday afternoon sales meetings lasted beyond five o'clock because it cut into his "happy hour" time. By the time March was winding down and the season was nearly upon us, we decided that his work ethic was definitely not conducive to what would be expected during the season, and we fired him.

We hired Vicky Aebersold to help supervise the concession operation. She had been with us for several seasons and was a hard worker, interested in getting into baseball on a full-time

*Sam, Peg Shaughnessy, and legendary manager Rocky Bridges at Municipal Field in Salem, Virginia.*

basis. She took on the added responsibility of cleaning the stadium after games.

We also hired Alfie Perdue. Alfie was another stadium employee interested in working in baseball full time. He had started with the club as a youngster, serving as a batboy before moving up to stadium maintenance, then concession work. He had helped oversee the concession operation the past two seasons.

Alfie's wife Patti also worked at the ballpark, selling tickets and tallying receipts at the end of each game. It was becoming quite clear that we would have to delegate much more responsibility to our better stadium employees to try to fill the void of not having a number-two person.

Several franchise changes had taken place during the off-season. The Prince William Yankees changed their nickname to the Cannons, although remaining a New York Yankee affiliate.

The Virginia Generals were sold to a group headed by Jay Acton, Eric Margenau, and Alan Levin, who were also owners of the South Bend franchise in the Midwest League and Watertown in the New York-Penn League. One of the first things they did was change the name back to the more popular Peninsula Pilots.

One other major franchise change also took place. The Hagerstown Suns moved into the Double-A Eastern League, and were replaced by the Frederick Keys. Both clubs were affiliated with Baltimore, with the Keys scheduled to move into a new ballpark in time for the 1990 season.

As our club opened its exhibition season at Pirate City in Bradenton, Florida, in late March, we received our first call from Rocky Bridges. It seems that Rocky, listed at 5'8" in his playing days, was concerned that we would order uniform pants too long for him. We assured him that we would make them fit, even if we had to have them altered after he tried them on. He still seemed concerned, but after a moment stated, "Ah, what the heck. You can't put earrings on a pig."

As soon as the team arrived in town, we held a luncheon to introduce them to our local media. During this gathering, Rocky went around the room introducing the members of the team. He then proceeded to tell a story about the Reverend Billy Graham speaking at Pilot Field in Buffalo the previous season while Rocky managed there. Rocky claimed he and Billy Graham had something in common. They both were able to get nearly 20,000 people at Pilot Field to jump up and holler "Jesus Christ".

As the season was slated to get underway, our roster contained the names of several players who had finished with us

*Carlos Garcia, a member of the '89 team who went on to the big leagues.*

the season before. Pitcher Keith Richardson, who had pitched so well for us in the play-offs, was one. Scott Ruskin had also returned, although he was being converted to a pitcher after having played first base and the outfield in each of the past two seasons. Carlos Garcia was our Opening Day short-stop. Among our newcomers, outfielder Moises Alou, the son of former major league player and current Montreal Expos manager Felipe Alou, was considered a top prospect. He had hit .313 with 7 homers, 62 RBI, and 24 stolen bases the season before at Augusta. His uncles, Matty and Jesus, also played in the big leagues.

Two highly touted pitchers also joined us for the first time, Randy Tomlin and Willie Smith. Tomlin posted a 7-5 record at Watertown in '88, with a 2.18 ERA. Smith was 1-4 with 6 saves at Augusta, but the Pirates were expecting big things from the 6'5" fireballing right-handed reliever.

Unfortunately, the weather failed to cooperate. For the first time that anyone could remember, all four Carolina League openers were rained out, not

*Randy Tomlin, a future big leaguer who was on our '89 team.*

once but two days in a row. It was an omen of things to come, as 1989 turned out to be one of the rainiest summers on record, especially in the Mid-Atlantic region.

The season finally got started, with four doubleheaders on what should have been the third day of the season. Highlighting that opening day was a seven-inning perfect game hurled by Dennis Burlingame of the Durham Bulls against Frederick. His teammate, Steve Avery, fired a two-hit shutout in the nightcap to complete the sweep for the Bulls.

On Sunday April 30th, we were playing an afternoon game at home against the Durham Bulls. Early in the game, one of the Durham players drilled a line drive home run over the right field wall and through the window of one of the homes located next to the ballpark.

A short while later, a police officer arrived at the park and demanded that we send a crew over to clean up the broken glass. I apologized to the officer but explained that all our employees were tied up, as we were in the middle of a ballgame. I told him we would be happy to send someone over as soon as things slowed down a bit.

The officer became upset and threatened to arrest me if I didn't send someone over right away. As Yogi would say, "It felt like deja vu all over again." Eventually I was able to make my point, getting the officer to agree to back off on my assurance that we would correct the problem as soon as possible. Within fifteen minutes I found an available worker and he cleaned up the glass.

On May 3rd our ace right-hander, Richardson, was promoted to Harrisburg. Richardson had started five games, posting a record of 4-0 with a 0.84 ERA. He had accounted for more than half our seven wins.

Tomlin then emerged as our top starter, picking up his club-leading sixth win on Sunday afternoon May 28th, at Kinston's

Grainger Stadium. The significance of that sixth victory was that it came on a no-hit, no-run, 1-0 performance. Tomlin was nearly perfect, allowing just two base runners, both reaching on infield errors.

Tomlin's no-hitter was the first by a Salem pitcher since 1975, when two were thrown. The first had occurred on April 11th, when Rod Scurry and Chet Gunter combined for eight innings of hitless ball in a 2-1 loss at Lynchburg. On May 27th Joe Neal no-hit Anderson for a 1-0 victory.

Even though the club was not winning consistently, we were getting some good individual performances from some talented players. Tomlin was named Carolina League player of the week for tossing his no-hitter. He was also named the Pittsburgh Pirates' minor league pitcher of the month for May. Former Buc Wes Chamberlain, now at Harrisburg, was named the Pirates' minor league player of the month for May. Our third baseman, John Wehner, was Carolina League batter of the week in early June, posting a .458 average.

On Saturday June 17th, we pulled off a promotional event that we had wanted to try for many years. We followed a ballgame with a concert. Things were messed up a bit when we were rained out the night before in Lynchburg, forcing us to play a doubleheader against the Lynchburg club the following night in Salem before the concert. However, we had already made provisions for just such a scenario.

We started the twin bill at 4 p.m., swept a pair from the Red Sox, then featured a performance by "The Platters", then "The Coasters". From a business standpoint, it was an extremely successful event. With the doubleheader, followed by a concert featuring two bands, we had over seven hours to entertain and, more important, feed the more than 4,400 fans who attended.

Knowing the potential that existed with this event, we instructed all stadium employees that none would be excused from work that evening. Unfortunately, despite the warning, both Alfie and Patti Perdue decided to attend the wedding of a friend before showing up about midway through the concert. I immediately fired both upon their arrival.

This created a great deal of negative feedback from a number of our regular fans who had known Alfie and Patti for years. They felt that I was unfair. But business is business. Had Alfie and Patti not stayed for the entire wedding reception they could have arrived at the ballpark on time. The welfare of the ballclub was not at the top of their list of priorities.

I took a lot of heat for my decision throughout the remainder of the season but would do exactly the same thing again if the situation presented itself. Baseball is my livelihood and I do take it seriously.

On a lighter note, on Saturday July 8th we hosted our third annual "Old Timers' Game". Headlining our event that day was Sparky Lyle, the American League Fireman of the Year in 1972 and American League Cy Young Award Winner in '77 - both while playing for the Yankees. Lyle had started his career with Boston, then played for Texas and Philadelphia after leaving New York. He retired in the early '80's.

Earlier in the day, Sparky attended a local fair while in town awaiting his appearance at our park. He spent much of his time at the dunking booth, trying to hit the target to knock the clown into the water. He tried and tried, but was unsuccessful, taking a tremendous amount of verbal abuse from the clown. As Sparky later confided to me, "Thank God that clown didn't know who I was or what I used to do for a living!"

The club played well in the first half, although we finished three games below .500 at 33-36. We ended up only two games behind first-place Lynchburg, and just a half game behind runner-up Frederick. Prince William finished on the bottom in

*Comparing handlebars . . . Sam and Sparky Lyle.*

our division. We entered the second half with a great deal of optimism.

We felt we had at least as much talent on this club as the two previous clubs that had appeared in the play-offs. Players like Alou, Garcia, and Wehner were solid. Pitchers Tomlin, Joe Pacholec, and, at times, Paul Miller gave us a good starting rotation. Our bullpen was strong, with Willie Smith, Blas Minor, and Joe Ausanio.

The Pirates were definitely supplying us with many talented players. The only problem was they were not leaving them together long enough to develop a winning team. Although we would like to win the title every season, it is important to keep things in perspective. Our role is basically to provide the opportunity to allow players to develop their skills, so that somewhere down the road they will be able to contribute to winning on the major league level. Some organizations believe that teaching their players to win in the minor leagues is an important part of player development and will carry over positively when they reach the major leagues. Other organizations feel the minor leagues are simply a place to provide players with the opportunity to hone their skills and learn the tools of their trade, with very little emphasis being placed on wins and losses.

Unfortunately for us, the Pirates had adopted the second approach, especially after the demise of Syd Thrift. It is difficult to argue with either philosophy, as each is exactly that — a philosophy. What really counts is the ultimate success of the major league franchise, and the Pirates were turning the corner toward respectability after several lean years.

As we moved into mid-July, our second-half optimism quickly faded when the Pirates promoted both Garcia and Alou to Harrisburg. Both had been tremendous defensively, as well as hitting third and fourth in our line-up respectively. At the time of the promotions, Alou was hitting .302 with a club-high 14 homers and 53 RBI. Garcia was at .283 with 7 homers and 49 RBI, along with 19 stolen bases.

It is also important that we keep in mind that advancement is also what it is all about for these players. Their goal is to eventually play in the major leagues, and one of our primary responsibilities is to provide them the outlet that will enable them to develop and improve their skills to advance to the next level.

On July 18th, the Carolina League All-Star Game was played at Durham Athletic Park. Kinston Indians shortstop Mark Lewis homered in the bottom of the sixth to lead the Southern Division over the North, 2-1. It was the second year in a row that the CL All-Star Game had ended up 2-1. Lewis also collected two other hits and was named the Most Valuable Player of the game.

Randy Tomlin, the starting pitcher for the North, worked two scoreless innings and allowed just one hit. Joe Ausanio also worked an inning in relief, allowing no runs and one hit. Our other two representatives also played, with catcher Scott Barczi going hitless in two trips to the plate, while John Wehner had an outstanding game. Wehner played the entire game, collected three hits in four at bats, and also made a spectacular defensive play at third base.

Both Carlos Garcia and Moises Alou had been voted to the All-Star team as starters, but both had to be replaced after being promoted.

July was a difficult month around the league from a weather standpoint. It was the wettest July on record in the Roanoke Valley, as we collected over 16 inches of rain. It seemed like we spent the entire month doing nothing but pulling the tarp on and off the field. Physically, my entire staff was drained.

In bad weather situations, the lower minor leagues are quite different from the major leagues or even the upper minors, where a full-time grounds crew handles the chores of preparing the field and covering the infield with a heavy canvas or vinyl tarpaulin during bad weather. In the lower minors, everyone in the front office becomes part of the grounds crew when the weather turns ugly.

Putting down an infield tarp usually requires about four to six people, even with the new, lightweight materials. Getting one up after a heavy rain can require as many as eight to twelve people, due to the added weight of the water that accumulates on the tarp.

Our grounds crew normally consists of one full-time groundskeeper and several part-time assistants. Therefore, whenever the rains start, our entire front office is on standby to

*A tarp covered Municipal Field. A depressing sight for a General Manager, but a common occurrence in 1989.*

assist with getting the field covered or the job would never get done.

As the season was winding down, it seemed like it would never stop raining. Everyone in our front office was exhausted because of all of the straining from putting the tarp down and getting it up. But had it not been for the tarp, we would have had many more than our five rain-outs, which was the fewest in the league. Both Lynchburg and Peninsula suffered fifteen postponements due to bad weather.

On August 4th, Tomlin was promoted to Harrisburg. He was leading the league with twelve victories. Not long after that, as our club was slowly sinking out of the pennant race, Rocky was asked to assess the club's chances.

"I've never seen a mule win the Kentucky Derby," was his response. As the club dropped further in the standings, Rocky

*The 1989 Bucks' Most Valuable Player John Wehner makes the throw across the diamond.*

said to me, "Well, Sam, the fat lady ain't singin' yet, but I sure can hear her hummin'."

Rocky was the one bright spot of the '89 season. He rarely got angry about anything, although I do remember his getting upset twice during the season. Both occurred when we were busy getting the tarp down after games because it was raining, and no one had taken him any beer. On each occasion he stood in the doorway of his office looking out at the field, wearing nothing but his cut-off long underwear and shouting, "Where's my ———' beer?"

We heard many of his lines during the course of the season. He told us about his new diet. He mixes two jiggers of rum with three cans of Ultra Slim-Fast. He said "So far I've lost five pounds and my driver's license."

He also told us that he had been a paid spectator at some pretty interesting events. He hastened to add that he'd always had a good seat on the bench too.

He had a classic line when asked by our local newspaper beat reporter near the end of the season what he was planning to do once the season ended. Rocky replied, "I'm going to go home and drink beer."

Despite ending the season with nearly the worst record in the league (seventh in the eight team league at 63-75) we placed four players on the end-of-season All-Star team. They were left-handed starter Tomlin, at 12-6, with a 2.35 ERA; reliever Ausanio, at 5-4, 2.12 ERA, and a league-leading and club-record 20 saves; outfielder Alou, who hit .302 with 14 homers and 53 RBI in just over half the season; and third baseman Wehner. Wehner hit .301 with 14 home runs and 73 RBI. He also stole 21 bases and led the league with 155 hits.

Not surprisingly, Alou captured the Buccaneer Player of the Month award in April, and Tomlin won for the month of May. Wehner received the award in June, and Ausanio won the award in July. Wehner was also named the Bucs' Most Valuable Player for the entire '89 season.

We also set a franchise attendance record for the third consecutive year, despite the rain and poor record on the field. We suffered through five rain-outs, and there were 27 other days when we played despite rain. We drew 121,581 fans to Municipal Field, surpassing the total of 119,966 set in 1988. Unofficially, the club set another franchise record with 51 tarp pulls.

Durham again led the league in total attendance, drawing 272,202 fans and setting another all-time Class A record for the second year in a row. In spite of the poor weather around the league, the league topped the one-million mark in attendance for the first time since 1947, with a total of 1,004,986 during the regular season.

Prince William won the second-half title in the Northern Division, while Durham captured both halves in the South. Prince William defeated Lynchburg, two games to one in the first round of the play-offs, then handled the favored Bulls, three games to one, to bring the Carolina League Championship to Prince William for the first time.

Durham's Grady Little was named Manager of the Year. It was the third time in his career that he had captured the award, winning it at Hagerstown in '81, then again with Kinston in '85.

Lynchburg's Phil Plantier became the sixth Lynchburg player in seven years to be named the Carolina League Most Valuable Player. Lenny Dykstra started the string in 1983, followed by Barry Lyons in '84, Shawn Abner in '85, Gregg Jefferies in '86, and Mickey Pina in '88. Plantier finished third in the league in hitting, with a .300 average, while leading the league with 27 homers and 105 RBI.

Frederick second baseman Luis Mercedes won the league batting title with a .309 average, the lowest average ever to win a C.L. batting crown. John Wehner finished second, at .301.

Charles Nagy of Kinston was named Pitcher of the Year, posting an 8-4 record with a 1.51 ERA before being promoted to Double-A around the middle of the season. The top draft pick in the June draft, Baltimore's Ben McDonald, made his pro debut in August for Frederick.

At the conclusion of the play-offs, I received a call from league president John Hopkins informing me that I had been voted the Carolina League Executive of the Year. Just several years earlier, I would have been ecstatic to receive such an honor, but not this time.

I asked John if I had to accept the award. He was somewhat surprised, but said, "If you don't want it, I'm sure we could find someone who does." I asked him if I could have a little time to think about it and he said to go ahead, but to call him right back.

I felt some resentment about not receiving any recognition in '86 or '87, when I felt I had worked harder than at any point

*Receiving the Carolina League Executive of the Year Award from league President John Hopkins at The Baseball Winter Meetings in Nashville, Tennessee in 1989.*

in my life. What we accomplished during those two seasons was incredible considering what we had to work with.

I believe I also had matured, now feeling that anyone who could survive in this business for any length of time had to be a hard worker and would also probably be as deserving of this award as I was. The award was not really important to me anymore.

I talked it over with my staff and they felt I'd be crazy not to accept it. After thinking it over, I felt that, from a publicity standpoint, it would probably be beneficial to our ballclub. I decided to accept the award on behalf of the club and let John Hopkins know. If nothing else, it made all those days pulling the tarp a bit more rewarding.

# 10 Ambushed!

As the season ended, our attention again turned to staffing. We were more stable in that regard than we had been, but we were still trying to find an assistant General Manager. Sam Clark vowed that he would not return on a full-time basis as our groundskeeper, so we also had another position to fill.

On the positive side, Dave Newman was planning to stick around for his third season as our director of broadcasting. Peg Shaughnessy was beginning her second season, and her title was changed from administrative assistant to director of marketing and community relations, to more accurately reflect her increased job responsibilities.

Vicky Aebersold had done an acceptable job in overseeing the concession operation and wanted the opportunity to work full-time in baseball. We felt she had proven to be deserving and added her to our full-time staff, assigning her sales responsibilities just like everyone else. She had no sales experience but felt she could learn. We probably spent more time trying to train her than anybody who had ever worked with us before. It turned out to be a losing battle. She tried hard but had problems communicating with other people. Unfortunately, in sales, communication is critical.

We worked with her up until opening day, even though she made little progress. We wanted to give her every opportunity to succeed. We also knew that once the season started, she would be back within her element at the concession stand and would be able to make a significant contribution to the ballclub.

In mid-November we were informed by Pittsburgh that our field manager for the upcoming season would be Stan Cliburn. We were disappointed that Rocky would not be back, but the Pirates felt they needed to place a greater emphasis on winning on this level, as the Carolina League had proven to be very competitive. The Pirates planned on using Rocky as a roving minor-league instructor.

Cliburn had led the Augusta Pirates to the South Atlantic League title in '89. Prior to managing at Augusta, he piloted the Watertown Pirates of the New York-Penn League in '88. Although just 33, Cliburn had caught for 14 seasons in the California, Atlanta, and Pittsburgh organizations. He appeared in 54 games for the California Angels in 1980. His twin brother Stu, a pitcher, also played professionally, including a stint with the Salem Pirates in 1977.

Several former Bucs players made news during the Baseball Winter Meetings in Nashville in December. Willie Smith was involved in a trade, going to the Yankees along with pitcher Jeff Robinson for Don Slaught. Pitcher Bill Sampen was left unprotected and was drafted by the Montreal Expos. The Pirates also lost reliever Jim Gott, who signed with the Dodgers as a free agent.

As we approached opening day, we hired Chad Kropff as our groundskeeper. Chad had worked for us as a grounds assistant in both 1986 and 1989 and was interested in becoming a full-time groundskeeper. In a reversal of roles, Sam Clark agreed to help out as Chad's assistant.

The only major change in the league saw the Peninsula Pilots sign a two-year working agreement with the Seattle Mariners. They had operated as a co-op team in '88 and '89, meaning that their players were basically supplied on loan from several different organizations. Actually, in '89 several of their players had been loaned to them by a Japanese team.

*The infamous scoreboard message center installed just hours
before Opening Day at Municipal Field.*

We also secured a one-line computerized message center
that we planned to add to our scoreboard. We had been pushing
our scoreboard company for several years after being promised
we would receive one if our attendance figures continued to
grow. With the opening of the new "Knights Castle" in Fort
Mill, South Carolina, to house the Charlotte Knights of the
Southern League, their old message center from Crockett Park
was available.

It was shipped to us, and the scoreboard company decided
to install it two days before Opening Day. Unfortunately, the
measurements they had taken previously to determine if it
would fit were incorrect. When they tried to put it under our
scoreboard, it was too wide. We needed to knock about a foot
of cinderblock off our outfield wall and we had just one day to

get it done. As if there were not enough things to worry about in preparation for Opening Day!

We called City Manager Randy Smith and explained our predicament. He sent a crew out the following morning and they worked with the scoreboard company for most of the day. When they finished, the message center was installed.

The technician from the scoreboard company worked all the next day, right up until game time, trying to get all the bugs out, and as the game started, the message center came to life. The average person showing up that night could never have imagined how close we came to not only having it not working, but almost not even getting it installed. Had it not been for a tremendous assist by the city, we never would have made it.

Later during the season, we began to feel we might have been better off without the message center. We hired Jon Kaufman to operate it, and he became creative. In fact, so creative that we got into trouble when he used it to question and criticize calls made by the umpires. He would also flash messages such as, "Morganna, you're needed in the club-house!" The fans loved his brand of humor, but it didn't sit well with Kelvin or John Hopkins.

One night the Kinston Indians brought in veteran relief pitcher Greg Ferlenda to try to close the door on a Buccaneer rally. Ferlenda had pitched for us back in 1986, then Hagerstown in '87, followed by Kinston in each of the next three seasons. As he was being introduced, Kaufman fed the message, CAROLINA LEAGUE LIFER, across the scoreboard. The Indians roving minor league pitching instructor, Dom Chiti, was in the stands and charged up to the pressbox demanding to know who put that message up? I took full responsibility and we had a heated exchange. His point was well taken, however, and we instructed Jon to lay off any future personal commentary relating to players or umpires.

We opened the season by sweeping a four-game series from Prince William at home, but things went downhill from there, with the club sinking to what was becoming our familiar basement position. Our hitters had started out on fire, however, and we could boast of having the Carolina League "Batter of the Week" for four of the first five weeks of the season.

Outfielder Greg Sims captured the honor in week one followed by Domingo Merejo, another outfielder, in week two. Chris Estep became our third outfielder to capture the award in week three when he went 8 for 20 with four homers and 10 RBI. Kinston's Jamie Allison interrupted our run in week four, but third baseman Bruce Schreiber regained it in week five by hitting .407 on the strength of a 13 for 32 performance.

On Sunday afternoon May 13th, in a game at Municipal Field, we entered the bottom of the eighth inning holding a 3-2 lead over Peninsula. Our catcher, Mandy Romero, led off the inning with a home run. Our team then proceeded to bat around and Romero came up again with two runners on base and clouted his second home run of the inning to tie a Carolina League record. When the dust had settled, The Bucs had scored nine runs en route to a 12-2 victory.

As we moved into the month of June, a number of our bigger special events took place. We opened the month with a big bang, literally, as the "Dynamite Lady" demonstrated her exploding routine on the field following a game. We followed that with our seat cushion giveaway, along with a number of other special events leading up to our June 16th "Baseball/Concert Doubleheader". With the success we'd enjoyed with the concert last season, we decided to try it again. This time we brought in "The Platters" and "The Drifters."

Unfortunately, this time things didn't go as smoothly. The 5 p.m. game between Salem and Kinston was moving along at a very brisk pace. We told the bands they should be ready to perform sometime between 7:30 and 8 p.m., based on an average game time of about 2 ½ hours. However, the game was flying along, and we had completed five innings in less than an hour.

"The Drifters" had arrived at our ballpark shortly before the game began, but "The Platters" had not yet arrived. We were getting concerned. Then a phone call from "The Platters" informed us that their van had broken down in West Virginia on their way in from Ohio. They were at a garage getting their brakes repaired and would not arrive for at least a couple more hours.

We knew the game would be over in less than an hour and told them to do their best to get here as soon as possible. The fact that "The Drifters" were already at the park gave us the idea of just letting them go on first and then having "The Platters" follow. When we suggested this to "The Drifters," they informed us that "The Platters" were doubling as their back-up band and without "The Platters," they had no music to perform to.

This really complicated things. We had no alternative but to wait it out and hope that "The Platters" would arrive before all of our fans left. We were also hoping the game would slow down or go extra innings but it didn't happen. The game ended in less than two hours and we informed the fans that there would be a minor delay. It was not even 7 p.m. yet and we weren't expecting "The Platters" until sometime after eight.

As 8 o'clock closed in on nine, some of the fans began demanding their money back and leaving. Fortunately for us, most were patiently awaiting the show. Finally, just before 9 p.m., "The Platters" arrived. It took them nearly another forty minutes to set up their equipment and check their sound, but the concert finally began. Those who had waited around were certainly pleased by the show, but it made us contemplate

*"The Drifters," performing at Municipal Field
on June 16, 1990.*

whether we should continue with this type of event in the
future. It's tough enough dealing with events that we have
much greater control over.

On June 20th, the first half came to a close. We posted the
worst record in the Northern Division at 25-45, finishing 14
games behind first place Frederick. Kinston nosed out Winston-Salem by one game to win the Southern Division first half
crown. At least we had the second half to look forward to.

One of the things that led to Syd Thrift's demise in Pittsburgh at the end of the '89 season was that he was spending
money on free agents to try to strengthen the club. When the
team slumped during the '89 season, members of the Board of
Directors felt that he was spending money unwisely, leading to
the power struggle and ultimate ouster.

The Pirates rebounded in 1990. As the major league season
was reaching the halfway point, Pittsburgh had opened up a

lead in the National League East and appeared headed for a division title for the first time since 1979. Many of the players playing big roles in the Pirates resurgence had been brought in by Thrift.

In late June, Peg Shaughnessy decided that she had had enough of the baseball life. She was homesick and lonely and informed me that she was leaving at the end of the month. I reluctantly accepted her resignation, although it left us short-handed at a very inopportune time.

She had done well for us, handling a number of administrative duties as well as sales. She was a quick learner and had made a strong contribution to our organization. But her family and boyfriend were back in her hometown of Framingham, Massachusetts, and after a little more than a year and a half of long hours, hard work, and little money, she finally decided to give it up.

As we moved into July, six of our players were named to the Northern Division All-Star team. The game was played at Prince William County Stadium. Catcher Mandy Romero, third baseman Bruce Schreiber, outfielders Chris Estep and Darwin Pennye, and pitchers Mike Pomeranz and Paul Miller were all chosen to represent Salem during the annual affair, won by the South, 5-4 in 10 innings.

Through the middle of the month, we remained in the race for the second half title despite playing less than .500 ball. Fortunately for us, everyone in our division was below .500 also. As we closed out the month of July, we fell out of contention after losing eleven games in a row. The losing streak fell two short of the all-time Salem record for futility, 13 in a row, set in 1982. Tim Wakefield halted the streak with a 2-1 victory over Peninsula.

The Pirates attempted to bolster our roster by sending in a number of new faces. Keith Richardson and Domingo Merejo

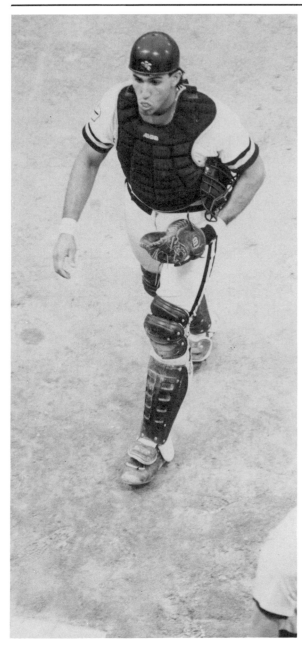

*Bucs 1990
team MVP
Mandy
Romero led
the Carolina
League
with 90 RBI.*

were returned to Salem from Harrisburg, and two first round draft picks, Austin Manahan and Willie Greene, were assigned to us from Augusta. Manahan was the Pirates' top draft choice in '88, while Greene had been the number one selection in '89. It was too little, too late.

During the season one of our players suffered a serious injury in a game at Municipal Field. Mike Brewington collided with Chris Estep in right center field while chasing a Texas league blooper. Brewington dived for the ball, catching Estep's knee just below his eye. His cheek bone was completely shattered, his nose broken, and his eye dislocated. He was rushed to a local hospital bleeding profusely and in a great deal of pain. Fortunately he was okay but his season was over. It would take him months to recuperate.

The incident brought back memories of a similar situation that had happened at Municipal Field near the end of the 1974 season. On nearly an identical play in almost the same exact spot, Salem right fielder Alfredo Edmead collided with second baseman Pablo Cruz. Edmead dived for the ball, and his head hit Cruz's knee as they came together. Edmead died as a result of the collision, suffering a massive skull fracture. It is one of only a few instances in all of pro-baseball history where a player died as the result of a game injury. A memorial plaque for Edmead is located under the grandstand roof near the press box at Municipal Field.

Many considered Edmead a legitimate major league prospect. The 18-year-old native of the Dominican Republic was in just his first season of pro baseball. He had so impressed the Pirates with his spring training performance that they'd sent him directly to advanced level Salem to begin his career.

He responded by hitting .318 with 7 homers and 61 stolen bases, combining with teammate and roommate Miguel Dilone for a total of 145 steals between them. Not surprisingly,

*Knuckleballer Tim Wakefield delivers the floater.*

Edmead along with Dilone was named to the end of the season Carolina League All-Star team just a day before the tragedy. Cruz was like a big brother to the young Latin players. Ironically, he had scouted and signed Edmead for the Pirates just a year earlier.

Late in the season, Hall-of-Famer Brooks Robinson headlined our fourth annual "Old Timers' Game". Ron Hodges, Bill Virdon, and Jim Holt also played in the game. Robinson was outstanding, participating in the game, then signing autographs for the fans after the contest.

We closed out the season by winning our final seven home games, as well as six of our final eight overall. We did it in exciting fashion, coming from behind in our last two games of the season. Chris Estep hit a three-run homer in the bottom of the ninth on August 29th to beat Lynchburg, 6-5. A two-run double by Domingo Merejo in the bottom of the ninth the following night gave the Bucs a 3-2 win over Lynchburg in the final game of the season. In that game, Bucs pitcher Chip Duncan set a Salem franchise record by recording 18 strikeouts in going the distance for the victory.

We still ended up with the worst overall record in the league, although we did manage to sneak into third place in the second half, just 6½ games out of first.

Mandy Romero and Bruce Schreiber were named to the end-of-season All-Star team. Both finished in the top ten in the league in hitting, with Romero at .291 and Schreiber at .290. Romero also led the league with 90 RBI, while he and Chris Estep tied for second in home runs with 17 each, just one behind league leader Greg Blosser of Lynchburg. Romero was also named our team MVP, narrowly edging Schreiber.

We set a franchise attendance record for the fourth consecutive season, attracting 126,121 fans to Municipal Field. In addition, for the first time in club history, we made it through the season without a single rainout. We were the only team in the league to play all 70 home games. We had plenty of rain, but our 29 tarp pulls was mild compared to the previous season.

Kinston captured both halves in the Southern Division, while Frederick took both in the North. In one of the most exciting final series in league history, Frederick scored six times in the ninth inning to win game one, 6-4. They also captured game three, 1-0 in 11 innings. With the best-of-five

*Pitching Coach Chris Lein studies the form of pitcher Chip Duncan, who struck out 18 batters to close the 1990 season.*

series tied at 2-2, Frederick rallied from a 5-0 deficit in the final game to win the Carolina League title, 6-5.

The Keys also drew 277,802 fans in their second season in the league and first in the new Harry Grove Stadium, to trail only Durham. Durham set a Class A record for the third consecutive season, this time drawing 300,499. The Bulls outdrew all 26 Double-A clubs, as well as 12 Triple-A teams.

Winston-Salem third baseman Gary Scott was named the league MVP, hitting .295 with 12 homers and 70 RBI. Ken Ramos of Kinston captured the league batting title by posting a .345 average. J.T. Snow of Prince William was named to the year-end All-Star team at first base, and Keith Mitchell of Durham was selected as one of the outfielders. The Manager of the Year was Wally Moon of Frederick.

Shortly after the season ended, I noticed Dave Newman in almost a catatonic state on several occasions. He apparently was having some type of problem. I called him into my office to discuss his situation.

He informed me that his wife had decided to end their relationship, and he was undecided about what he wanted to do. He asked for a few days off to go back to his native Chicago area to talk with his brother, a minister. Later that week he resigned his position to return to Chicago to live. I tried to persuade him to stay, but his mind was made up. We would once more begin searching for an announcer.

In meeting with Vicky Aebersold, we came to the conclusion that sales was just not her thing. We would be unable to keep her around during the off-season unless she handled advertising accounts. We had replaced Peg Shaughnessy late in the season with Karen Carter, and now Karen and I were all that was left of our staff, following Chad Kropff's move to Florida to take a job with our former groundskeeper, Murray Cook at West Palm Beach, shortly after our season ended.

Cook had left Harrisburg a short while after accepting that position to go to work for the City of West Palm Beach, Florida, overseeing their baseball facility, home to the West Palm Beach Expos of the Florida State League. It was also the spring training base for both the Montreal Expos and the Atlanta Braves.

I was beginning to feel that all of my time was being spent looking for and training new employees. As soon as we became comfortable with someone, it seemed we would lose them for one reason or another. I was willing to give just about anything for a stable and competent staff.

The first step in this regard would be finding a solid number-two person who was interested in staying around. We decided to concentrate all our efforts on finding just such a person before looking for another announcer or groundskeeper.

I started calling some of my closer friends at other clubs to get some input on who might be qualified and looking to make a move. I called Marty Nash to see if he had any suggestions. Marty had moved from Miles Wolff's Burlington club to his Durham Bulls prior to the '89 season. He had just completed his second season as the Bulls director of sales and marketing and everything was going incredibly well for him and the Bulls.

He mentioned that he had recently heard from Dennis Robarge, the General Manager of the Elmira Pioneers. Dennis had called to see if he knew of any openings with a full-season team, as he was interested in advancing beyond the short season New York-Penn League. Marty gave me his phone number and I called him.

Although I didn't know a lot about Dennis, I had talked with him on several occasions at baseball seminars and the Winter Meetings. He was likeable and had a good attitude as well as solid knowledge of the baseball business.

Even though he was the General Manager in Elmira, his responsibilities more closely resembled those of an assistant General Manager. He worked directly under the club owner, Clyde Smoll, who had purchased the Elmira club from Bobby

Bragan at the end of the '86 season. Smoll was a hands-on owner, working out of the club office on a daily basis.

Dennis had spent the '88 and '89 seasons in Elmira as the assistant General Manager before being named General Manager of the club in 1990. Prior to that, he spent four seasons with the Little Falls Mets, starting as their play-by-play announcer in 1984. It was approaching mid-October, and we were interested in getting together to see if we could work things out. I suggested that he come to Salem to look at the area.

Dennis, his wife Amy, and young daughter Katie made the trek down and met with Kelvin and me on a Friday. They spent the better part of the weekend looking around and meeting some of the park employees during a staff gathering on Saturday. Before leaving the gathering Saturday night, Dennis informed me that he would accept the position.

We felt we had finally solved our biggest staffing problem. It would take a tremendous burden off me. Dennis assumed his new job in early November. We were happy to finally land a strong number-two person. Unfortunately, there was little time to celebrate. A problem of great significance that had been slowly developing over the course of the previous year appeared to be coming to a climax.

The major league clubs had just announced that they were pulling out of the Winter Meetings scheduled for Los Angeles during the first week of December. They were reacting to the minor leagues' refusal to ratify a one-year interim agreement in an attempt to resolve a stalemate over a new Professional Baseball Agreement. There was even some talk that the major leagues would refuse to supply players to the minors in 1991.

The Professional Baseball Agreement, the rules that bind major and minor league baseball clubs, including the standard player-development contract defining the relationship between the major league club and its minor league affiliate, was set to expire on January 12th.

The previous agreement, reached in 1986 for a five-year period, had required very little negotiating, and both sides quickly agreed and ratified it. That agreement was similar to its predecessor, except that each minor league club saw a significant increase in the amount of money paid to them for "special considerations" by their major league affiliate. The "special considerations" money basically was an indemnity fee paid by the majors to the minors for infringing on their markets via national TV broadcasts.

Prior to the first negotiating session in July, most had felt that a deal similar to the last two would be worked out, with the possible exception being even more "special considerations" money for the minor leagues due to the huge TV contracts that major league baseball had just entered into.

But a couple of events had taken place near the end of the '89 Winter Meetings in Nashville that were causing some concern. First, Commissioner Fay Vincent had called a meeting with the minor league presidents to demand improved salaries and working conditions for minor league umpires.

The second was a vote taken and approved by the minor leagues to change the title of the president of the National Association of Professional Baseball Leagues, the minor leagues governing body, to "Commissioner" of minor leagues. Apparently Fay Vincent felt threatened by the new title bestowed on Sal Artiaga, although most minor league people felt the change was more ceremonial in nature, rewarding Artiaga for his service to the minors.

In the Spring, Vincent accused the minor leagues of failing to respond to his request, then issued a warning to minor league owners regarding the upcoming negotiations. Apparently, a line was being drawn. When the bargaining teams met in July to set an agenda for the negotiations, there were no indications that any radical changes were being planned. In August, both sides exchanged their first proposals.

The major league proposal called for a comprehensive set of facility standards that most minor league clubs could not presently meet. It also did away with all "special considerations" payments and instead required the minor leagues to begin paying the majors up to $150,000 per club to receive players. In addition, the major leagues would assume total control over all player transactions, as well as doing away with the transaction fees paid by major league baseball to the N.A.P.B.L. The N.A.P.B.L. had been paid an administrative fee to keep records of all minor league player moves. The major leagues would also have the right to approve all minor league franchise sales and transfers, as well as all minor league expansion and league schedules.

The minor league proposal called for very little change from the previous agreement, with the exception of asking for a large increase in "special considerations" money, as expected. The major leagues responded by terminating all 59 working agreements due to expire at the end of the 1990 season, of which ours was one.

No meetings took place in September, but when talks resumed in early October, a deadline of October 24th was imposed by the major leagues.

Dick Wagner, the former GM of the Reds and Astros, was named by major league baseball as the new "director of minor league player development". His job was to implement a contingency plan for a new minor league system starting in 1991.

The general consensus around the minor leagues was that we were very poorly prepared for these negotiations, and basically had been ambushed! The N.A.P.B.L. executive committee walked away from the table on October 24th due to a lack of any progress being made.

Dan Ulmer, a Louisville banker and the president of the Louisville Redbirds, had previously worked on a number of business deals with Carl Barger, the president of the Pittsburgh Pirates. Both had been involved in the negotiations, and Ulmer was anxious to work something out. After the talks broke off, Ulmer was designated by Artiaga to meet with Barger. They worked out details of a one-year interim agreement, but when the N.A.P.B.L. failed to ratify it, the major leagues pulled out of the Winter Meetings.

The N.A.P.B.L. executive committee had decided that the agreement would not be approved by the minor league owners and began working on a new proposal. At a meeting in Chicago on November 17th, the N.A.P.B.L. approved a package that included most of the demands made by the major leagues and submitted it to the major league owners for approval.

At the same time, the minor league owners created a committee to look into ways to supply players to the 59 clubs that had lost their major league affiliations, and voted to begin lobbying Congress to look into the way major league baseball was treating the minor leagues.

The major league owners met in Chicago for their own separate version of the Winter Meetings, while all minor league people went ahead with plans to gather in Los Angeles during early December. On the eve of the split Winter Meetings, the N.A.P.B.L. plan was rejected by the major league owners.

Walking around the lobby of the Westin Bonaventure Hotel in Los Angeles felt much like walking around a funeral home. Unlike the normally festive atmosphere associated with Winter Meetings of the past, the mood was somber.

There was  dissension even among our own ranks; one side seemed to be willing to do whatever it would take to come to an agreement with major league baseball, while the other side felt we should hold our ground and call their bluff, believing they needed us as much as we needed them.

Negotiations continued via telephone during the Winter Meetings as Ulmer and Barger tried to iron out their differences in the language of the agreement. Although not all details were completely resolved, the N.A.P.B.L. executive committee unanimously approved the package via conference call on December 7th.

The Winter Meetings were about to end, and there were mixed emotions on both sides. Each league was scheduled to vote by fax on December 13th for final approval, and the agreement was expected to pass. I felt that as a group we were totally unprepared, and as a result had been forced to accept a package that was not in our best interest. We had given up too much.

The agreement was for a seven-year period with either party having the right to reopen negotiations after September 30th of the third year. If reopened, the agreement would be voided if no subsequent agreements were made by September 30th of the fourth year.

The major league clubs gained nearly everything they were looking for, including the right to approve franchise sales, relocation, and schedules of their minor league affiliates. They also limited the number of games each minor league classification could play. Many of the facility standards were also implemented. The burden of nearly all travel expenses was placed on the minor league clubs, and the major leagues assumed the administration of all player contracts and eliminated the transaction fees paid to the N.A.P.B.L.

Most important, the "special considerations" money for television rights would no longer be paid by the major league clubs but, instead, each minor league club would begin paying up to five percent of its gross ticket revenue to major league baseball. The minor leagues were forced to guarantee a flat fee of $750,000 in 1991, a minimum of $1.5 million in '92, $1.75 million in '93, and $2 million in '94. What a complete turn around!

In exchange, the major leagues agreed to pick up all equipment expenses and player meal money, most of which they already were responsible for. The only major gain for the minors was a guarantee of players for all existing minor league clubs that wanted them.

On December 13th, the new Professional Baseball Agreement was ratified. The major league owners had unanimously approved it, but the minor league owners were not as overwhelmingly in favor. A three-quarters vote was needed, and that's exactly how the vote turned out, 27-9 in favor. The voting was very close in several leagues, and three full-season leagues voted against it. The Carolina League was one of those opposed.

*Pittsburgh Pirates Parrot getting friendly with Sue Lazzaro.*

# 11 Grinding Ordeals

Although we were opposed to the new agreement from the outset, we were in the minority and had no choice but to accept it once it was ratified. We would have to make the most of it and began looking into ways to hold down expenses while increasing revenues to offset the money we anticipated losing as a result of the agreement.

On a positive note, the Pirates had won the National League East title in 1990. Even though they were beaten by the Cincinnati Reds in a tough six-game National League Championship Series, they were now favored to win the NL East again in '91. Shortly after the new agreement was approved, we locked in a new four-year affiliation with the Pirates, carrying us through the '94 season.

Just before Christmas, we hired Mike Minshall as our new director of broadcasting. He had recently worked for the Chattanooga Lookouts of the Double-A Southern League as a back-up announcer. He came on board after the holidays to assume his new role.

In late January we were informed by the Pirates that Stan Cliburn would be back as our field manager in 1991. Our new pitching coach would be Tom Dettore. Dettore had spent nine years in pro baseball as a player, having reached the big leagues in '73 with the Pirates and then playing for the Cubs from 1974-76. His lone claim to fame was giving up one of the longest home runs in Wrigley Field history to Dave Kingman.

As we approached the start of the season, several improvements were made to the stadium. The home clubhouse and manager's office were upgraded, and the press box was expanded to four times its previous size to accommodate a major college baseball tournament that we would be hosting during the spring in conjunction with the City of Salem.

Sam Clark agreed to handle the groundskeeping chores on a temporary basis until we could find somebody else. He hired a couple of part-time helpers and began training them as his successors.

Several weeks before the start of the season, Karen Carter resigned. She had been having trouble with her sales duties. With the season nearly upon us, there was little time to train a new person, but we got lucky when Mike Baum applied for her position. Mike had recently graduated from nearby Virginia Tech and was now enrolled in their Sports Management Masters Program. He was from the Virginia Tidewater area and had worked for the Tidewater club previously as a stadium employee.

We hired him and he immediately made an impact. He worked hard and, although his aggressiveness at times rubbed people the wrong way, he was able to get things done. He missed out on our pre-season advertising sales, having joined us just as the season was getting started, but he jumped into ticket book and group sales with a great deal of success.

For the first time ever, we also brought in two interns. Dennis worked out an arrangement with Roanoke College, which is located in Salem, to accept one of their students starting in May. I had also met with a student from Virginia Tech interested in working with us as an opportunity to get his foot in the door of pro baseball.

Our staff was finally beginning to take the shape we had been striving for. With our front office staff and two interns, we had six men working in the front office. Along with Sam Clark and his two assistants, we had a total of nine men available for tarp duty. This was a luxury we had never known. It was so easy now that we actually looked forward to pulling the tarp.

We opened the season at home on April 11th with the largest opening night crowd in franchise history. The total of 3,127 surpassed our previous best of 2,361 set in 1989. We followed that with a crowd of 5,534, believed to be the largest second-night crowd ever for the club. Unfortunately, we lost both games to Winston-Salem.

Two even bigger losses took place the next two days, a Saturday and Sunday, as the rains came and washed out both contests. With record-setting crowds the first two nights, the last thing we needed was to lose an entire weekend to the rain. We had made it through the entire previous season without a single rain out, and now had two in our first four games. The club then went on the road for a week.

Even though the team was not playing particularly well, hovering just below the .500 mark, several individuals were beginning to emerge as potential stars. Kevin Young, Rich Aude, and William Pennyfeather got off to quick starts with their bats. On the mound, Paul Wagner, and Steve Buckholz were performing well as starters, with Dave Tellers pitching extremely well out of the bullpen.

On May 13th the club hit the road for a week, and we prepared to host the Metro Conference Tournament with a berth in the NCAA regionals guaranteed for the winning team.

The Metro Conference included the team that had been ranked number one in the nation for most of the season, Florida State. Also playing out of the Metro Conference were South Carolina, Tulane, Memphis State, Southern Mississippi, Louisville, Cincinnati, and the host school, Virginia Tech.

The tournament was scheduled to begin on Wednesday, May 15th. Tuesday was media day, with each club getting an opportunity to work out on our field and meet with media representatives covering the tourney. We planned on using Monday to put the finishing touches on the field for the tournament.

On Monday morning we received a phone call from Danny Monk, the Associate Athletic Director at Virginia Tech. He informed us that a game between Cincinnati and Florida State over the weekend had been protested and the protest had been upheld. That meant the game would have to be resumed at the point of protest and completed before the start of the tourney because the game would have a bearing on the tourney seedings. They would have to play at our park that afternoon.

During the playing of the protested game, we ran into our first rain shower. We stopped the game and covered the field until the rains stopped a short while later. Unfortunately, this was just the first of what seemed like an entire week of nothing but on-and-off rain.

At the conclusion of the game, the rains came again and we put the tarp down once more. The forecast called for more rain overnight, so we covered the field again as the sun went down, meaning we would have to be back in the park at around 6:30 the next morning to get it up, unless it was still raining. If a tarp is left on the grass after the sun comes out, it takes only about twenty minutes for the tarp to absorb enough heat to seriously burn the grass. At 6:30 the next morning, the entire staff was assembled at the ballpark, and we removed the tarp once more. Before media day was over, we had put it down and taken it up again. The forecast once more included a chance of overnight showers, leaving us no other option than to cover the field again overnight. We did get some heavy rain during the night, but it cleared off by morning and we removed the tarp and began the tournament.

There were several well-played games during the day, but the evening game was interrupted by rain, forcing us to put the tarp down once more. It felt as if Mother Nature was just playing with us, trying to see how much we could take. Nearly as soon as we would get the field covered, the rain would stop and we would have to take the tarp up again.

Virginia Tech lost to South Carolina in a slugfest the opening night of the tourney. The Hokies lost again the next afternoon, eliminating them from the double elimination event. Losing the host team would not help attendance.

The final night game was a long one, and it also included the brief rain delay, making it a very late night at the old ball yard. We left during the wee hours of the morning, again having covered the field before departing. Just several hours later we were back to uncover the diamond and start another set of games. It was grueling!

Between the raindrops and tarp pulls, we eventually managed to get to the finals. Florida State had been knocked into the losers' bracket by Southern Mississippi, and the Metro title would hinge upon their rematch on Sunday afternoon.

We again covered the field at the conclusion of the games on Saturday night, and on Sunday morning we awoke to a light drizzle that persisted for much of the day. The game was to start at 2 p.m., but neither coach wanted the title to be determined by the weather. We sat around for a couple of hours beyond the scheduled starting time, while the rain kept lightening up, then drizzling a bit harder.

Finally, the coaches and conference commissioner decided to cancel the game and declare the teams co-champions, feeling both had a chance at being invited to the College World Series regionals, which is exactly what happened.

The team had played a seven-game homestand just before the Metro Tourney, and we had spent the entire week of the tournament practically living in the park. Immediately upon the conclusion of the tournament, we started another seven-game homestand, followed by a brief four-game road trip, then three more games at home. Hosting 31 games in less than four weeks had taken a toll on the entire staff. It wasn't something we were looking to do again right away.

First baseman Ben Shelton had a big month of May, posting a .280 average with 10 homers and 37 RBI. Pitcher Tim McDowell, the son of former Indians' star "Sudden Sam" McDowell, also had a good month, winning three of four decisions, including a shutout, while compiling a 2.70 ERA. Dave Tellers picked up four wins and a save to go with his 1.25 ERA.

As we moved into the month of June, the club remained in the pennant chase, although still playing below .500 baseball.

On Saturday June 8th, with the Bucs again on the road, we hosted the Virginia State Group A High School Baseball Championship. This was a piece of cake compared to the Metro Tourney, but still one more event to keep everyone busy while our team was out of town.

On Monday June 10th, we received a call from the Winston-Salem club asking how the arrangements were progressing on our "Baseball/Concert Doubleheader" scheduled the following Saturday. They were concerned, explaining that they were working with the same outside promoter and their concert had fallen through.

I was uneasy after the conversation and immediately called the promoter. We were planning on bringing in "The Shangri-La's" and "The Drifters" for our third annual Summer Beach Concert. I had a difficult time reaching him and, when I finally did, he began making all kinds of excuses as to the problems he was running into.

I told him that we had a contract with him to deliver those bands and had already paid him several thousand dollars to guarantee the show. He assured me that he would still be able to make the show happen. I was skeptical.

Although this was the third year in a row that we had presented a concert in conjunction with a ballgame, it was the first time we had worked with this particular promoter. The previous promoter did not have a particularly good reputation, but he had ultimately delivered the goods.

We had switched to this new promoter, Bob Jones, because he was a former minor league baseball executive and seemed better able to relate to our particular needs. Ater a number of conversations, he convinced me that he could put together the type of show we wanted, and we were happy with his oldies line-up of "The Shangri-La's" and "The Drifters". It had the potential to be our best show yet.

Shortly after receiving Jones' assurances that the show would take place, we received another call from the Winston-Salem club. They had come up with a phone number for the manager of "The Shangri-La's" and had talked with him just before calling us. He had informed them that he knew nothing about this appearance and no contracts existed.

Not wanting to believe what we were being told, I called the manager myself. He told me exactly the same thing. No concert was planned for his band this coming weekend. He did inform me that he remembered having heard from Bob Jones several months before and that Jones had asked him to send a contract for the date in question, but the contract had never been returned.

It was Monday afternoon and our show was supposed to take place on Saturday, just five days away. There was no way we could make the necessary travel arrangements and come up with the type of back-up band needed to bring in "The Shangri-La's" on our budget. "The Drifters" were yet another story.

The manager of "The Shangri-La's" gave me the phone number of "The Drifters" manager, who informed me that his group was booked in Washington, D.C. for the upcoming weekend. He, likewise, knew nothing about an appearance in Salem or any other ballpark in the coming weeks. The show was definitely not going to happen!

I called Jones again and revealed this new information. He was apologetic and offered to refund our deposit. I told him we were interested in salvaging a show at this point, as we already had a pretty good number of advance ticket sales. He said he'd see what he could come up with, but by now we weren't about to depend on him for anything.

I locked my office door and spent the better part of the next two days on the phone trying to put together a show that would be comparable to the one originally planned. I also called Kelvin, who brought our team attorney into the picture. It was a bad situation.

I didn't sleep well for the remainder of the week, feeling that I had let the club down. I had trusted this promoter and had been burned. I felt upset and betrayed.

By Wednesday, we had come up with a show that we felt would be acceptable, considering the circumstances. We would bring in "The Platters" and "The Foundations". We then went public with the information surrounding the change. A local newspaper reporter called and I explained the situation to him. He began questioning me about bringing suit against the promoter. I told him he would have to talk with our club attorney about that, and he said he would.

A short while later I received a call from Kelvin. He was very upset at me for telling this reporter that we were planning to sue the promoter. I told him that I never said that and asked where he got the information. He said the reporter had just talked to our club attorney and told him that I said it. Now I was even more upset about the developments. I immediately called the reporter, demanding to know why he would tell our attorney that I had said something that I hadn't.

He replied in a very matter-of-fact tone that our attorney refused to tell him anything so he told the attorney that I made that statement to try to get him to respond.

I told him I didn't think that was ethical and thanked him for nearly costing me my job. He apologized for the inconvenience, but made no offer to explain his tactic to Kelvin or our attorney. I was miffed.

The week had certainly been educational. First it was the promoter, then the reporter. I was beginning to feel that there was no one I could trust. This ordeal had certainly taken its toll, especially following so closely behind the physically grinding Metro Tourney. For the first time since getting into baseball, I had serious thoughts of getting out!

On Thursday afternoon we ran into one more problem relating to the concert. A local agent from the Virginia Alcoholic Beverage Control Board paid us a visit to inform us that our beer license was good only for professional sporting events. We would not be allowed to sell beer during our concert on Saturday.

We tried to explain to him that the concert was just an extension of the baseball event, with only one admission charged for both, and we had been allowed to sell beer during the concerts the previous two seasons. He told us that it was an oversight on their part, and would not happen again. The only recourse we had was to get the law changed at some point in the future.

At least the concert did take place, even though we had to cut off beer sales immediately upon the conclusion of the game. Most people there were upset by the ruling and many left before the concert even began.

*The Budweiser Clydesdales take a stroll*
*around Municipal Field.*

I'm not an advocate of drinking, but I feel that in a controlled manner it has its place. If someone wants to sip a cool brew on a hot summer evening while watching a ballgame or listening to pleasant music in an outdoor setting, that is his or her prerogative.

We pride ourselves on having had no major alcohol-related incidents in our park since my arrival. We train all of our people in the serving or dispensing of beer. We want people to have fun in our park, but we also want them to feel safe. I feel we do a good job of accomplishing both.

From a business standpoint, selling beer is important to us. All the more reason to take the precautions we do. We can't afford not to sell beer, as it accounts for approximately 40 percent of our concession revenue each season. Therefore, we're going to do everything within our power to protect our beer license.

We eventually received a refund check from Bob Jones' concert promotion company, but the check bounced. We filed a claim through the court system in Ohio where they were based, but never received our money. What a great company to work with!

The team slumped during the final week of the first half, going 2-5 to finish at 30-40. We ended up in third place, eight games behind Prince William in the Northern Division. Kinston again finished on top in the South.

As the second half got underway, third baseman Kevin Young and catcher Keith Osik were promoted to Double-A Carolina. The Carolina Mudcats had become Pittsburgh's new Double-A affiliate after the Harrisburg Senators opted to hook up with the Montreal Expos at the end of the 1990 season.

Young had been among the top ten hitters in the league all season long. He was hitting .313 at the time of his promotion. Mike Brewington was also released. He had returned to action with our club after suffering that very serious injury, but was never able to make much of a contribution.

We started the second half strongly and entered July in first place. Ben Shelton was leading the league in home runs and RBI in early July when he received the call to report to Carolina.

On Monday, July 6th, we were at home to host the Frederick Keys. Righthander Erik Schullstrom was on the hill for the Keys. He had hurled a no-hitter against Kinston in his last outing, and hadn't allowed a home run in 36 2/3 innings.

In the bottom of the first, our lead-off hitter grounded out. Then our next batter, Roman Rodriguez, hit his first home run of the season. Paul List, Alberto De Los Santos, and Ken Trusky followed with home runs to make it four in a row, equaling a feat accomplished only one other time in the 47-year history of the Carolina League, on July 11, 1984, by Kinston.

On July 3, 1989, our club had hit four homers in one inning against Lynchburg but they weren't consecutive. This new record, however, meant that our club had now become the only team in league history to twice hit four home runs in one inning, and both had come in the past three seasons.

One night while our team was out of town, I was settling into bed just after 11 p.m. when I received a call from the Salem Police Department. They had apprehended two people inside the stadium and wanted to know if we wished to press charges. I asked if they had vandalized or tried to steal anything? I was told that they hadn't.

I was then informed by a very sheepish officer that the two were a man and woman. I hadn't yet caught on to what the officer was embarrassingly trying to explain. It seems that the man was a big baseball fan and had this fantasy of making love on a baseball diamond. The couple had scaled our fence for the purpose of living out his fantasy but were apprehended prior to carrying out the act.

I was relieved to find out that it wasn't a typical case of breaking and entering. I told the officer to issue a stern warning, but we had no desire to press charges. He then let them go.

The Carolina League All-Star Game was played in Frederick on July 24th. It was an important game for us, as we would host the All-Star contest in 1992 and looked at this as an important opportunity to devise the strategy for our event.

Mike Baum attended the festivities primarily to take notes on everything that went on. Kelvin, Dennis, and I also attended. Frederick featured a re-creation of the "Field of Dreams" infield scene with a mock cornfield surrounding their diamond, followed by an Eddie Rabbit concert and fireworks on their field the night before the game. It was a spectacular show.

We placed three players on the Northern Division All-Star team, pitchers Dave Tellers and Paul Wagner and outfielder

*Former Pirates pitcher Bruce Kison delivers to the plate during our "Old Timer's Game" on Aug. 8, 1991. Also in the picture, former Oakland A Jim Holt and umpire Wally Moss.*

Daryl Ratliff. Tellers was promoted to Carolina prior to the game and was replaced on the squad by Tim Edge, our catcher. The game was won by the South, 6-5.

We remained in first place as we entered the month of August. On August 8th, Willie Stargell headlined our fifth annual "Old Timers Game". "Pops", now a roving instructor with the Atlanta Braves, made an appearance and signed autographs during the event. In 1988, Stargell had become only the 17th player elected to the Baseball Hall of Fame during his first year of eligibility. We concluded the night with a bang, as "Captain Dynamite" did his thing by exploding in his "coffin of doom" following the ballgame.

Had it been our choice, we would have preferred to see our pitching coach climb into that "coffin of doom" instead of "Captain Dynamite". Tom Dettore had been a real problem all season long. He seemed to enjoy aggravating people, and it was something he was very good at.

It started with a baseball camp he planned to conduct at our park. He planned to charge youngsters for a day of instruction, even though this was something we normally provided free. He wanted us to advertise and promote his event, and used one of our interns to print and distribute flyers all over the area. He promised to pay the intern if the event made any money. He also gave us permission to sell our team souvenirs in the park during his camp if we paid him a percentage of our sales. What a nice guy!

Because he was charging for a service we normally provided free, we were reluctant to support it. He assured us that he had permission from both Kelvin and Chet Montgomery, the Pirates' minor league director. We found out later that Kelvin was not in favor of this camp for the same reasons we objected to it.

Only about a dozen youngsters signed up, and when we received a brief morning shower, it gave Dettore an excuse to cancel it.

One afternoon in late May, while out on the field removing the tarp after a brief shower, we heard Dettore yelling as he charged across the field toward us. He was upset, mumbling that he was planning to sue the City of Salem. He wanted to know if we knew anyone that could "fix" a speeding ticket.

He claimed he was "set up" by the police, who had a speed trap nearby. He had been stopped and given a ticket.

I asked, "How fast were you going?"

He replied, "A little over 50."

I was puzzled, "Isn't the limit 35 in the area where you were ticketed?"

He said "Yes, but that's beside the point. They set me up, and I'm going to sue them."

*Willie Stargel (left) talking about old times
with former teammate Bruce Kison (right)
as Bucs' first baseman Mark Johnson (center) listens intently.*

I wished him luck, and we resumed rolling the tarp.

In July he demanded that I give him a dozen team caps. When I refused, he claimed the Pirates had authorized it and that I'd better comply. When I again refused, he started pounding his fist on my desk, trying to intimidate me.

I just looked at him, smiled, and said, "I don't have a dozen caps to give you and I wouldn't even if I had them without getting authorization from Pittsburgh myself."

He then stormed out of my office, babbling something to the effect of "Isn't my word good enough?"

After he left, I called the Pirates and was assured that they had not and would not authorize anything of this type. The caps belonged to the Salem club, not the Pirates. What we do with them is our business, I was told.

We had more incidents with Dettore than one could imagine. When we asked him to play in our "Old Timers' Game" he refused, asking, "What's in it for me?"

When our team photographer tried to take his picture for our team baseball card set, he walked away, saying, "I don't want my card in the set unless I'm getting paid for it."

Around the middle of August we received a call from our bank. They wanted to know if we knew someone named Tom Dettore. He had gone to the bank to cash a check, and when asked to show some identification, refused and became belligerent. By the time he left, the teller was practically in tears, prompting the call to my office. We apologized for his behavior but we certainly weren't surprised by it.

As the season was winding down, we were informed of another incident involving Dettore. On one of our final bus trips he decided to light up a cigar as he sat in the seat directly behind the driver. He kept blowing smoke at the driver, trying his best to aggravate him.

The driver asked him politely several times to stop blowing smoke in his direction as it was bothering him and making it difficult to drive the bus. Dettore just laughed and intensified the behavior.

Finally, the driver pulled over to the side of the road and refused to go any farther until Dettore put out his cigar. It turned into somewhat of a stalemate as Dettore continued puffing away. Eventually, Dettore decided that he wasn't interested in spending the entire night sitting on the side of the road and relinquished the cigar.

With about two weeks left in the season, the Lynchburg Red Sox moved ahead of us into first place in our division. We had lost a number of players due to injuries and moves, but still managed to stay in the race. We were only three games out, with three games left, when we traveled to Lynchburg to close out the season. We needed to sweep the Sox to finish in a tie for the top spot. We dropped the first game of the series and the race was over.

We finished up at 63-77 overall, placing us sixth in the eight-team league. Our second half record of 33-37 put us four games behind first-place Lynchburg. We led the league with a team batting average of .263, and outfielder Paul List finished second overall, at .318, trailing Lynchburg's Jeff McNeely (.322). Daryl Ratliff and Alberto De Los Santos both finished in the top ten in the league in hitting.

Outfielder Scott Bullett, who arrived in Salem in late July after being promoted from Augusta, posted a .333 average. He was named our player of the month for August, and on August 31st was promoted to Pittsburgh, becoming the first player in recent memory to be promoted directly from Salem to the major leagues.

A pitcher named Hector Fajardo was with us briefly before working his way to the majors earlier in the season, but, unlike Bullett, he made stops in both Carolina and Buffalo before advancing to Pittsburgh.

The Peninsula Pilots won their final game of the season! That may not seem like such a big deal, but the win snapped an all-time league record 22-game losing streak. The previous record had been set by Fayetteville early in the 1950 season when they lost 19 in a row.

In the play-offs, Lynchburg beat Prince William, two games to none, to win the Northern Division Title. Kinston won both halves in the South, then swept Lynchburg in three straight to capture the championship.

Kinston's Mike Soper set a Carolina League record by recording 41 saves. The 41 saves also tied the minor league record set by Mike Perez of Springfield in the Midwest League in 1987.

Brian Graham of Kinston was named Manager of the Year, Sam Militello of Prince William, at 12-2 with a 1.22 ERA, was named Pitcher of the Year, and the Most Valuable Player in the league was third baseman Pete Castellano of Winston-Salem. Castellano hit .303 with 10 homers and 87 RBI.

Despite having four rain-outs in '91 compared to none in 1990, we set a new franchise attendance record for the fifth year in a row. We ended the season by drawing 131,582, to surpass our previous best by more than 5,000. The Frederick Keys drew 318,354 to break Durham's Class A record, set in 1990. Durham also broke its old record by attracting 301,240 to Durham Athletic Park.

The season had been both physically and emotionally draining. We were definitely looking forward to a vacation. It had been a tough year.

# 12 An All-Star Affair during Our Silver Anniversary

Dennis had gone through some tough times away from the job as well, especially late in the season. He and his wife Amy were not getting along, and he decided to move out and look into a separation. She then moved back to New York State, taking along their young daughter Katie. Dennis had been extremely close to Katie and this separation hurt him very much. Eventually he and Amy divorced.

On a positive note, the Pittsburgh Pirates were coming off another strong season in '91, having captured their second straight National League East crown. The Bucs had finished a comfortable 14 games in front of second-place St. Louis.

A number of former Salem Bucs had made heavy contributions to the major league club. First baseman Orlando Merced and third baseman John Wehner spent much of the latter part of the season manning the infield corners. Merced began the season with only 25 games of big league experience, but his flair for the dramatic made Pirates' fans quickly forget about the departed Sid Bream, who had signed as a free agent with Atlanta.

Merced hit .275 with 10 home runs and 50 RBI, and seven of his ten homers either tied or won games. He finished second behind Jeff Bagwell of Houston in balloting for the National League Rookie of the Year. Another former Buc, Wes Chamberlain of the Phillies, finished fifth in the balloting.

Prior to a late-season back injury, 1991 had been a dream season for John Wehner, as he compiled a .340 average while playing spectacularly on defense.

Randy Tomlin also played a big part in the Pirates' second straight division title, posting a record of 8-7 with a stingy 2.98 ERA, leading the Pirates in that category. Stan Belinda contributed 16 saves after setting a Pirates rookie record for saves in 1990.

The Pirates fell once more in the National League Championship Series, this time to the Atlanta Braves in a tough seven-game series, after leading three games to two.

On October 30th, Mark Sauer was named the Pirates' new President and CEO, replacing the recently departed Carl Barger. Barger had taken over the top spot with the new Florida Marlins, scheduled to begin play in 1993.

Also in October, the first meeting of the "Roanoke-Salem Baseball Hall-Of-Fame" committee took place. The committee was put together by area veteran American Legion baseball director Posey Oyler in response to a conversation I'd had with Bob Teitlebaum about forming a local organization to honor area players, coaches, and contributors to the game of baseball.

The committee assembled by Oyler was a good one; both Kelvin and myself were included along with Oyler, who was elected the first president of the organization.

Three sportswriters were also included, Bob Teitlebaum and Jack Bogaczyk, of the *Roanoke Times & World News*, and Brian Hoffman, the Sports Editor of the *Salem Times-Register*.

In addition, Ron Hodges, the ex-New York Met catcher and an area real estate agent, Wayne LaPierre, an accountant, Carey Harveycutter, the manager of the Salem Civic Center, which currently houses the Hall of Fame as well as our annual hot stove banquet, John Rocovich, a prominent attorney and avid baseball fan, and Ed Via, a writer and equally big baseball fan rounded out the committee.

After defining the purpose of the group and setting up a charter, we decided to induct up to five people in our inaugural

*Dave Parker accepting his "Roanoke-Salem Baseball Hall-of-Fame" plaque at Municipal Field in 1992.*

ceremony to be held in late January. To be eligible, the person had to be from, or have played, coached, or supported baseball within the seven-county area making up and surrounding the Roanoke Valley.

The first five inductees were Dave Parker, a former Salem player who captured the Carolina League MVP Award in 1972, Al Holland, a Roanoke native who played for the Salem Pirates before moving on to a fairly distinguished big league career, Billy Sample, a Salem native who played in the major leagues, Fletcher "Kid" Carr, a former area semi-pro player and long time scout, now 84 years old, and Walter "Steve" Brodie, a

Roanoker who compiled a lifetime .308 career major league batting average while playing from 1890 until 1902. Brodie passed away in 1935 at the age of 67.

The Baseball Winter Meetings were held in Miami Beach in early December and the gathering was a bit more festive than the Los Angeles gathering the year before. Two former Bucs were involved in a trade during the Miami Beach convention, when Scott Ruskin and Willie Greene were sent from Montreal to Cincinnati. Both had been traded from Pittsburgh to Montreal along with Moises Alou on August 8, 1990 for pitcher Zane Smith.

Other than that, the Winter Meetings were much more laid back and enjoyable. We spent as much time as possible just walking the beach and relaxing. It was much needed after the season we had just endured.

We were gearing up for the upcoming season with what we felt was the best front office staff we had ever assembled. Mike Baum was doing extremely well in sales and had also been instrumental in bringing our front office into the computer age. He possessed outstanding computer skills and was able to improve the computer skills of everyone else in our office.

Dennis had taken a tremendous load off my back by handling many of the day-to-day operations, freeing me to handle more of the administrative details which had become much greater due to our growth and success.

Mike Minshall was making a strong contribution in sales, in addition to his broadcasting skills. He also enjoyed designing and laying out ads and put together both a "25th Anniversary " and "All-Star Game" logo for the upcoming season. Sam Clark again bowed out, once more insisting that he would not return to handle the grounds in '92. We hired a replacement for him at the Winter Meetings. Our new groundskeeper, Jeff Sennett, joined us shortly after the first of the year.

We also added another full-time front office person, hiring one of our interns from the previous summer. Dave Shonk had done a tremendous job handling every task given to him and was interested in a full-time position after graduating from Virginia Tech. He was our first choice to fill the newly created opening.

The 1992 season would be very big for us. In addition to hosting the All-Star Game on July 22nd, we also planned to tie a number of events into our "Silver Season" celebration throughout the year, marking our 25th season in the league.

In late January we introduced our new field manager for the upcoming season, John Wockenfuss. Wockenfuss had played for the Detroit Tigers and Philadelphia Phillies, breaking into the big leagues with Detroit in 1974. He spent twelve years in the majors, compiling a .262 lifetime batting average. His best big league season was in 1980, when he hit .274 with 16 homers and 65 RBI for the Tigers.

Wockenfuss had also managed previously for four seasons in the Tigers farm system, starting in 1987 at Lakeland in the Florida State League. From there he jumped to Class Double-A Glens Falls in the Eastern League in '88 where he piloted the team to a regular season championship. The Tigers promoted him to Toledo of the Class Triple-A International League in '89, where he remained until being let go early in the '90 season. He did not work in baseball in '91.

Fortunately, we were also assigned a new pitching coach. It's a good thing, because our bus company had already informed us that they would not be interested in transporting our club had Dettore returned. Our new pitching coach was Rick "Buster" Keeton, a former pitcher for the Milwaukee Brewers, who had spent the '91 season in the same role at Augusta.

On the big league level, the Pirates made a change in general managers. Larry Doughty was relieved of his duties, although no specific reason for his dismissal was given other than that he had made some mistakes, and it was felt that the club was headed in the wrong direction.

He made a number of trades, giving up young players believed to be prospects. He also lost Wes Chamberlain and Julio Peguero by inadvertently placing them on waivers, only to have them claimed by the Phillies. To try to cover the mistake, he made a mock trade, sending Tony Longmire with them to Philadelphia for Carmello Martinez.

On February 5th, Ted Simmons became the Pirates new Senior Vice President and General Manager. Simmons had worked with Mark Sauer in St. Louis, where he was the farm director for the Cardinals. He promised a strong commitment to player development and the minor leagues.

As the Pirates opened spring training in Bradenton, Florida, 13 former Salem Bucs were on the forty-man roster, including Ben Shelton, Scott Bullett, and Daryl Ratliff from our '91 club. The percentage had grown each season since reuniting with Pittsburgh in '87.

We opened the season on the road, traveling to Peninsula and Kinston. In the season opener at Peninsula on April 9th, we were no-hit on a combined effort by Greg Bicknell and Chuck Wiley. The Pilots also took the next two games before we finally broke into the win column in our fourth game of the season. The team then traveled to Kinston for a series before returning home on April 16th.

The night before our home opener, we played host to a college game between Virginia Tech and the University of Virginia. In addition to hosting the Metro Conference Tournament in '91, we had also begun hosting at least one Virginia Tech game each year, starting in 1990 when Tech played Florida State at our park. It has become a good relationship, increasing the exposure of the Virginia Tech program in the

*Two Salem Mayors, Leonard Shank (left) and Jim Taliaferro,*
*throw out the first pitch on April 16, 1992,*
*to commemorate our 25th season in Carolina League.*

nearby Roanoke market, and giving us an opportunity to generate additional revenue.

To celebrate our 25 years in the Carolina League, our home opener took on the flavor of our first CL season, 1968. We aired a 1968 flashback show over our public address system as the gates opened, and also had a display of 1968 classic cars. Both the current Mayor of Salem, Jim Taliaferro, and the Mayor in '68, Leonard Shank, were on hand for the first pitch ceremony. Mr. Shank, now in his 90's, really enjoyed the opportunity to go out on the field and take a bow.

We won our home opener against the Durham Bulls, then struggled, closing our first homestand at 2-5. We battled rain on six of the seven days, although only one game was postponed. However, opening the season with a number of tarp pulls had taken its toll on our new groundskeeper. As the team headed out of town for a week, Jeff disappeared.

After several days of not seeing him around, we began to worry. We found his stadium keys locked in the maintenance shed, causing us even greater concern. We had no idea where he was or what had happened to him, and upon checking his apartment, discovered it vacant. It was several weeks before he finally called from his home in Wisconsin to say that he couldn't handle it anymore and had to leave. I thanked him for the courtesy of giving us plenty of advance notice.

After his disappearance, we hired Sam Clark's brother Eric. Eric had been our groundskeeper for parts of the '85 and '86 seasons, and had been Jeff's assistant prior to his vanishing.

The Bucs swept Prince William on the road in late April, finally reaching the .500 mark at 9-9. Rob Bailey and Rich Aude had gotten off to quick starts offensively, and both were among the league leaders in the early going.

The club remained near .500 as we moved into May. On Thursday May 14th we were scheduled to open a four-game series at home against Winston-Salem. Unfortunately, the weather refused to cooperate. We had completed only the first inning when the rain hit, forcing us to postpone the remainder of the contest.

On Friday, heavy rains returned, forcing another postponement and requiring us to schedule doubleheaders on both Saturday and Sunday. On Saturday we were finally able to resume play, picking up the suspended game in the top of the second inning. We completed two more innings before heavy thunderstorms rolled in again, forcing another postponement.

We would now have to complete the suspended game on Sunday, followed by a doubleheader. In essence, we would be playing only the second triple-header in Carolina League history. The first had taken place nearly nine years earlier, on August 6, 1983, when Hagerstown swept three from Durham in a similar situation.

After a gloomy Sunday morning, the sun came out and we were finally able to play ball. We picked up the suspended game in the fourth inning, but lost, 12-5. The club then bounced back, sweeping the next two, 2-1 and 4-3, to take two of three on this unusual day. The fourth and final game of the series would be made up in Winston-Salem as part of a doubleheader later in the week, as we would not play them again at home during the first half.

Several players who started the game on Thursday were not around at its conclusion on Sunday. Designated hitter Genero Campusano was released, while third baseman Bruce Schreiber and outfielder Tom Green were both promoted on Friday.

On May 28th, I had a major confrontation with John Wockenfuss. It wasn't the first time I'd ever gotten into an argument with a manager, and I was sure it wouldn't be the last. But this argument was much more heated than any I'd ever been involved in before.

We had an early morning shower and Wockenfuss called the office and left the message that the club was tired and banged up, and could use a night off. We had heard the same thing from him several times in mid-May, and again at the start of this series. The thing that upsets me most when a manager starts complaining about not wanting to play, is that it shows a total lack of consideration of our responsibilities. It is important to both the franchise and our fans that we play whenever possible, because it is our responsibility to generate as much revenue as possible for the franchise. After all, unlike many retail establishments and restaurants, we have only 70 opportunities to play at home each season.

It is also important for a manager to condition his players to perform day in and day out. This is certainly something they will have to be prepared for if they make it to the major leagues, where games are rarely postponed any more by the weather, and the season is nearly a month longer.

Because we were shorthanded, I was helping the grounds crew prepare the field before the game when Wockenfuss came out of the clubhouse to check the field conditions. When he was unable to find anything wrong with the playing surface, he became upset and started jumping all over Eric Clark about his groundskeeping, complaining that he hadn't put down enough diamond dry a few nights earlier.

I immediately came to Eric's defense. Wockenfuss then blew up at me, telling me that neither of us knew anything. He then started complaining that I hadn't given the team enough batting practice balls. I tried to explain that if he needed more balls he should call the Pirates because they were responsible for providing balls.

I also tried to say that the office staff never questioned or tried to tell him how to do his job and would appreciate the same courtesy.

By this time he wasn't willing to listen to anything and started waving his arms around, cussing, and calling me names. I thought he was going to take a swing at me, but he eventually backed off and stormed into the clubhouse.

Here we were, working our tails off doing our jobs. Having to put up with this nonsense made me wonder whether it was all worth it. We played that night, and the following day Wockenfuss apologized for his behavior. From that point on we got along pretty well.

As already recounted in Chapter 6, I do remember one time when a manager's request to cancel a game was valid. It was the early season game in '86. We had opened the gates despite a stiff arctic wind, snowflakes in the air, and only one fan, Robley Stearnes, had shown up in full Eskimo attire.

It didn't take much persuading for Mike Bucci to convince me that we would be better off trying to play two the following night, and even the die-hard Stearnes didn't object to the postponement. Unfortunately, the weather didn't improve much, and we were blown out in both games the following night in front of 133 hardy (or foolish) spectators.

Although the team never made a run for the top spot, we remained in the hunt until the final week of the first half. We enjoyed solid pitching for most of the half, but had little offensive support. When the hitters produced, the pitching wasn't there. We finished the half at 33-36, in third place, six games behind first-place Lynchburg and two behind runner-up Frederick.

Peninsula and Durham, with identical records of 37-32, finished in a dead heat for the top spot in the Southern Division. League by-laws dictate that a first-half tie will go to the team that wins the first meeting between the two clubs in the second half. That distinction went to Peninsula.

On June 30th we encountered some heavy morning rain and the field took quite a bit of water. The sun came out later in the day, and I spent most of the afternoon on the field raking and helping our grounds crew prepare for the game that night. We had been experiencing unseasonably cool weather for much of June, but on this day the mercury took a dramatic climb after the rain stopped.

The following morning, as I was at home getting ready for work, I began to feel dizzy. I dropped to my knees and could feel myself losing consciousness. I called to my wife, then the next thing I remember was waking up on the floor with my wife trying to talk to me. She had called 911, but by the time the local rescue squad arrived, I had regained my senses and was feeling okay.

The squad checked my vital signs and felt I was fine, except for my blood pressure being a little high. They offered to take me to the hospital but I refused. They then recommended that I see a doctor to be sure nothing was seriously wrong. I agreed to do so, then headed off to the ballpark to prepare for our game that night.

At my wife's insistence, I did see a doctor the following day and he found nothing wrong. In discussing the circumstances surrounding my losing consciousness, he felt that it was probably a combination of dehydration and exhaustion and recommended that I slow down a little and not push myself so much.

On July 4th, the team was on the road, and Kelvin invited my family to spend the day at his home on nearby Smith Mountain Lake. My sons love to swim in his pool and, as always, we had a relaxing, enjoyable time.

The following morning, a Sunday, I was relaxing and reading the paper at home when I again began to feel dizzy. This dizziness was followed by chest pain, heart palpitations, shaking, and profuse sweating. I feared that I was having a heart attack.

I tried lying down but started feeling even worse. I told my wife to call 911. Being a Sunday and a holiday weekend to boot, the rescue squad that arrived appeared young and inexperienced.

As I lay on my bed in the midst of what I felt was a heart attack, I heard a member of the rescue squad talking into his radio, saying he didn't think they could handle the situation and didn't know what to do. This really made me feel good! My chest pains and heart palpitations increased, and I demanded that they get me to a hospital as quickly as possible so that I could be treated by someone who knew what was going on!

I was rushed to the emergency room and a doctor and nurses began connecting all types of electrodes to my body. They were monitoring my heart to determine if I was, in fact, having a heart attack. After reading a number of monitors and running some additional tests, the doctor informed me that my heart was fine.

He asked me some questions, including several about my job, then informed me that he felt my problem was stress-related. He told me that I needed to pace myself better, slow down, and find ways to relax. He recommended I see a doctor specializing in stress management, then wrote me a prescription for a mild anti-anxiety medication and told me to go home and get some rest.

The medication helped and, shortly thereafter, I began seeing a doctor to learn to manage stress. He told me that I definitely have a type A personality, and people with type A personalities are very desirable employees because they tend to get things done. I just needed to channel all that energy in a positive direction, and step back and take a deep breath whenever feeling tense or uptight.

I also learned that stress is cumulative, and that very rarely is an attack like mine caused by a single incident. More often than not, many stressful occurrences over a period of time tend to build up and can then be triggered by some additional setback.

In retrospect, I could look back at a number of things that might have contributed to my problem. All of the worry related to staffing, the strain of the Metro Conference Tourney, the problems with the concert promoter, along with the everyday pressures of event management and the uncontrollable problems with the weather and club performance.

In many ways, this incident may have been a blessing. Although it took months before I felt fully recovered, I immediately changed a number of bad habits.

Being a non-smoker and non-drinker was a positive to begin with. Although I drank coffee only in the morning, I was drinking much more than I needed. I started drinking nothing but decaffeinated from that point on.

I also changed my diet and eating habits dramatically, eating more fruits, vegetables, and whole grain foods, while cutting back on all meats, especially red. I stopped snacking on chips and sweets and undertook a strenuous exercise routine including bike riding, jogging, and brisk walking. In less than a month, I dropped over 20 pounds. Since I was only slightly overweight to begin with, I now felt better than ever.

As July progressed, we were approaching the Carolina League All-Star Game and everything was coming together nicely. This would be the fifth time Salem had hosted this event in 25 seasons in the league.

The first was in the club's inaugural season of 1968. At that time the club with the best record would host the best players from the rest of the league. The front-running Salem Rebels defeated the Carolina League All-Stars, 6-1, in only the second C.L. All-Star Game ever played outside the state of North Carolina up to that point. Some notable players who appeared in that game were Wayne Twitchell, Gene Tenace, Tony Soliata, Joe Lis, Carlos May, Charlie Sands, and Frank Baker.

Salem hosted its second C.L. All-Star contest in '74. It was a slugfest, as the All-Stars outscored the Salem Pirates, 14-9. Four Pirates hitters connected for round trippers, including a three-run shot by Steve Nicosia. Todd Cruz, Don Aase, John Candelaria, and Mitchell Page appeared in that game.

Just two years later, in 1976, the Carolina League All-Stars hosted the Triple-A Charleston Charlies at Municipal Field. The All-Stars posted an 11-5 win behind Salem pitcher Ed Whitson, who started the game and picked up the victory. The game featured several former Salem players on the Charleston team, including Miguel Dilone, Craig Reynolds, Ken Macha, and Mitchell Page.

The most recent time Salem played host to the event was in 1984, after the game had evolved to pitting the Northern Division against the Southern Division. In that game, the South won easily, 11-6, as Luis Quinonez went three for five for the winners. Stan Jefferson homered for the North, while his Lynchburg teammate Dave Magadan collected three hits. Jim Traber also picked up a pair of hits in the losing effort for the North. Other notable players appearing in that game were Cecil Fielder, Felix Fermin, Bip Roberts, Barry Lyons, and Mike Greenwell.

Our 1992 event was turning into an extravaganza. It would become the first Carolina League All-Star Game ever televised on a regional basis, being broadcast on both the SportSouth and Home Team Sports Networks, reaching a potential of five million households.

We held a banquet at the nearby Salem Civic Center the night before the game, with Salem native Billy Sample as our featured speaker. We also held a concert following the banquet with country music singer/comedian Johnny Russell putting on an excellent show.

But it started raining during the concert following the banquet, and our staff left to go to the ballpark to cover the infield with the tarp. Unfortunately, Eric failed to turn off the sprinkler system and the sprinklers came on underneath the tarp the next morning. The field was soaked despite being covered during the overnight shower. The rains continued on and off throughout the day, but fortunately we caught enough breaks between raindrops to make the field playable. It rained hard late in the afternoon but almost miraculously let up again shortly before game time, enabling us to start on time.

We placed three starters on the Northern Division squad: shortstop Ramon Martinez and outfielders Keith Thomas and Midre Cummings. All of the night's festivities came off extremely well, our advance ticket sales were strong, and we anticipated a good crowd for the game.

The game was well played and exciting, with the host Northern Division picking up a 5-2 win. The Most Valuable Player was our own Midre Cummings, going two for four with a double and an RBI.

Shortly after the conclusion of the game, the skies let loose again with heavy rain throughout the night. It was as if someone upstairs had been looking out for us, providing us with just enough of a window to get the game in.

Once that game was behind us, it was a tremendous load off our entire staff. We had spent hundreds of hours planning and preparing, starting a year earlier in Frederick. Despite the rain on the day of the game, we still drew 4,219 fans, far and away the largest crowd to ever attend a Carolina League All-Star Game in Salem. The biggest event of our "Silver Season" was successfully behind us, and we were pleased.

*In 1992 Midre Cummings hit .305
and was MVP in the Carolina League All-Star Game.*

The Durham Bulls came to town the following night to open a three-game series. We had been swept by them in Durham a few weeks earlier, and there was some bad blood, as the team felt that they rubbed our noses in it when they beat us 20-3 in the final game of the series. In that game, the Bulls' second baseman Hector Roa homered, dropped his bat and stood at home plate watching the ball leave the park, then very slowly and tauntingly, pranced around the bases.

The first game was uneventful, but late in the second game, Roa charged the mound after dodging the third pitch thrown at his head that evening. Both benches emptied and the war was on. Over the years, we've seen many baseball brawls, but few could compare with this one. It got ugly! Four players from each team were ejected, along with John Wockenfuss.

Usually after an altercation of this magnitude, everyone is on their best behavior. But the following night, the hostilities resumed. This time things were even more violent. Seven players and both managers were ejected, and the Salem Police were called in to provide protection for the Durham club as they boarded their bus after the game. It was the first time we ever had fans telling us how disgusted they were with the activities on the field. As a result of the fights, both managers and fourteen players were fined.

As we moved into August, the team stayed close to .500, but was never able to put together any type of consistent streak to make a run. The player moves had continued again through-out the season, making it difficult to gain any type of momentum. No team in our division was overwhelming and that kept everyone alive for most of the half.

On August 8th, we hosted our 6th annual "Old Timers' Game". We were very lucky in securing a headliner, as Dave Parker had taken ill in late January and missed his induction into the "Roanoke-Salem Baseball Hall Of Fame", but we were

*Dave Parker and Sammy Lazzaro after the "Old Timers' Game" at Municipal Field in 1992.*

able to persuade him to come to town to accept his plaque and play in our game.

Parker had been active as a major league player just the season before, but had been released upon its conclusion. No one had offered him a contract for the '92 season, but he was still interested in playing and looked to be in great shape.

We really didn't know what to expect from him because we were told that he probably would not be overly cooperative. In a phone conversation prior to his appearance, he informed us that he would not sign autographs. We tried to talk him into it, even offering him additional money, but he held firm.

Maybe it was because of all of the warm memories that came back to him once he returned to Municipal Field, but Dave Parker was one of the most cooperative players to ever appear in our "Old Timers' Game". He was friendly and courteous to everyone there.

He played in the game, then ended up signing autographs for many of the youngsters, although refusing to sign for most adults. Overall, we were impressed with him. He commented that his season in Salem, 1972, was the turning point of his career. It was the season that convinced him, as well as many others, that he could play in the big leagues. He captured the Carolina League MVP Award and nearly won a triple crown, leading the league with a .310 average and 101 RBI, while his 22 homers were only one behind league leader Robert Gorinski of Lynchburg. He later went on to win the National League MVP Award in 1978.

Al Holland made his first appearance in our "Old Timers' Game" as well. In 1983, he posted 25 saves for the Philadelphia Phillies and was named Co-Fireman of the Year in the National League. Holland played for Salem in 1976, compiling a 4-2 record and a 2.96 ERA.

We finished the second half with a record of 31-40, in the basement, 9½ games behind Lynchburg. Peninsula edged Winston-Salem by a half game in the South to sweep both halves, just as Lynchburg had done in the North. Peninsula then completed their "worst to first" season by downing Lynchburg, three games to two in the championship series, after finishing with the worst record in the league in '91.

Leading the Pilots to the title was league MVP Bubba Smith. His 32 home runs were the most hit in the league since Gerald Davis hit 34 for Salem in 1981. Smith also drove in 93 runs. Peninsula pitcher John Cummings was named Pitcher of the Year with his 16-6 record, while Pilots manager Marc Hill was named the top manager.

Our own Ramon Martinez was named to the year-end All-Star team as the top shortstop. He also captured our team MVP Award, hitting .289 with 35 steals while playing spectacularly

*Roanoke-Salem Hall of Fame Board of Directors: (from left)*
*Brian Hoffman, Jack Bogaczyk, John Rocovich, Ed Via, Ron*
*Hodges, Carey Harveycutter, Wayne LaPierre, Sam Lazzaro,*
*Posey Oyler, Bob Teitlebaum, Kelvin Bowles.*

at times on defense. Outfielder Midre Cummings finished fifth
in the league in hitting, with a .305 average.

Despite ending up with the worst record in the league, we
set a franchise attendance record for the sixth consecutive
season, drawing 134,598. We were also informed that our
string of ten consecutive years of attendance growth ranked
number one in all of pro baseball.

In spite of another disappointing year on the field, from a
business standpoint, our "Silver Season" had been a good one.
The All-Star event came off exceptionally well, and the fact
that it was televised by two major networks was a definite asset
for the league.

**13** **Rebuilding Again**

Now that we had finally assembled a quality staff, the big trick would be keeping it together. Unfortunately, our first defection took place shortly after the season ended.

We shut our office down for a week to allow everyone a much-needed vacation. Just after we returned, Mike Minshall informed us he had accepted a job with the Quad City River Bandits of the Midwest League.

Although the Midwest League is actually a step below the Carolina League, the owner of the Quad City club, Richard Holtzman, also owns Chattanooga, a Double-A team, and Tucson, a member of the Class Triple-A Pacific Coast League. Minshall felt that the move would provide him a much better opportunity for advancement.

We also encountered a problem with Eric Clark around the same time. Over the years, Eric has had problems with gambling, and a number of 900 calls to gambling "tip lines" had shown up on our telephone bill. Eric insisted that he did not make the calls, but they had been made from the stadium press box at a time only Eric had access.

To avoid a long, drawn-out investigation, we accepted his resignation in lieu of the several hundred dollars owed to the club for the calls. He never admitted making the calls but, based on the evidence, felt he had little chance of clearing himself.

So much for keeping our staff together. The season had been over for less than a month, and already two of our six permanent staff members were gone.

One other noteworthy happening took place right after our season ended. On September 7th, Major League Baseball Commissioner Fay Vincent was forced to resign. The move was precipitated by a September 3rd meeting in Chicago in which the owners voted to ask for his resignation. Basically, the owners appeared to be making Vincent the scapegoat for the economic problems the game was facing.

Not many minor league people were heartbroken over this development. We had felt it coming for a while, and we were still upset at the stance the Commissioner had taken during our recent negotiations with the major league people over the new Professional Baseball Agreement. He had fired the first shot, and that was still fresh in our minds.

On the major league playing field, the Pirates captured their third straight National League East Division crown, finishing nine games in front of runner-up Montreal. The Atlanta Braves again captured the title in the West, setting up a rematch of the '91 National League Championship Series.

It was another great confrontation, with the Pirates battling back from a 3-1 deficit to take the series to a deciding seventh game in Atlanta. Unfortunately for the Pirates, they were unable to protect a 2-0 lead, as the Braves rallied in the bottom of the ninth. Who will ever forget Sid Bream sliding across home plate just under the tag of Mike LaValliere, following a two-out pinch hit by Francisco Cabrera, to win the series in dramatic fashion!

The Pirates had lost Bobby Bonilla to free agency after the '91 season, yet still managed to win another pennant. The big question at the end of the '92 campaign was whether the Pirates would be able to re-sign Barry Bonds and Doug Drabek, as both were eligible for free agency.

Several more former Bucs played key roles in the '92 Pirate pennant drive. Pitcher Tim Wakefield won a combined 20 games between Class Triple-A Buffalo and Pittsburgh, including a major league mark of 8-1 with a 2.15 ERA. He also picked up two wins in the National League Championship Series against the Braves.

Paul Wagner, who played in Salem in both '90 and '91, went 2-0 with a 0.69 ERA after being called up late in the season. John Wehner, however, suffered through an injury-plagued season, appearing in only 55 games. He hit just .179 following his incredible showing the year before. Kevin Young had also been called up late in the year after playing in Salem just a season earlier. He hit .571 in limited action, and the Pirates were expecting big things from him in the future.

In late September the Carolina League approved the sale of the Peninsula franchise to a group including former New York Mets shortstop and manager Bud Harrelson. The Pilots had been one of the worst draws in the league for a number of years, including the past season, despite capturing the league championship. Harrelson's group purchased the club from Jay Acton and Eric Margenau for a reported $1.6 million.

One of the conditions of the sale was league approval to move the team to Wilmington, Delaware, where plans were underway to build a new stadium in time for the '93 season. As a result of this move, a realignment of divisions was necessary, with Wilmington moving to the Northern Division where they would fit in better with Frederick, Maryland, and Prince William, located in northern Virginia. Lynchburg would also remain in the North, while we would move to the South to join Durham, Kinston, and Winston-Salem.

In addition, the new Wilmington club would be affiliated with the Kansas City Royals instead of Seattle, and the Winston-Salem Spirits also switched parent clubs, going from the Chicago Cubs to the Cincinnati Reds.

On November 5th, the Pirates announced that Scott Little would be our field manager in 1993. That's right! The same Scott Little that played such a big part in our '87 championship season. As a player, Little had advanced to Class Triple-A Buffalo and was briefly called up to the Pirates. But in '91 he became a player-coach at Buffalo, and the following season was named manager at Augusta.

On December 1st, the day before we left for the Baseball Winter Meetings in Louisville, Kentucky, the Houston Astros announced the signing of pitcher Doug Drabek. The big talk during the meetings was what Barry Bonds was going to do. Bonds was present in Louisville, and an announcement was expected before the meetings ended.

On December 8th, our final day in Louisville, the San Francisco Giants announced that they had reeled in the prize catch of the free agent market with the signing of Bonds. With the loss of Drabek and Bonds, the Pirates had lost two more key players. An even greater burden would be placed on the young Pirates prospects to produce in '93.

Except for the signing of Bonds, the Winter Meetings were uneventful. The only other major topics of discussion were the extremely cold temperatures outside in Louisville during that first week in December and Jesse Jackson's appearance in protest of baseball's hiring policies, brought on in part by racist statements attributed to Marge Shott.

Even though we had two job openings to fill, we decided not to pursue them during the Winter Meetings. We had already made several contacts with regard to the groundskeeping position and were confident we would fill it soon.

As for the radio job, we had received dozens of tapes and resumés without even announcing the opening. The thought of being paid for watching and talking about baseball games is apparently quite appealing.

Another reason we decided to forgo an employee search at the Winter Meetings is that they have become a virtual meat market for prospective job seekers. The number of people attending each year in search of a job has increased to an unbelievable level, making it difficult to sift through all of the resumés in a timely manner.

Unfortunately, hundreds of people spend a great deal of time and money trying to land that elusive first job in baseball, when each year, only a few low-paying jobs for the most part are offered.

On the morning of December 9th, we packed our luggage and made the seven-hour return drive to Salem. Upon arriving home that evening, we learned via newscasts of the death of Florida Marlins' President Carl Barger from a heart attack during an owners meeting in Louisville earlier in the day. It was shocking!

I didn't know Mr. Barger well, but had met him at several Pirates functions over the years when he headed the Pittsburgh club. He was one of the major players in the negotiations in 1990 over the new Professional Baseball Agreement and was instrumental in breaking the impasse. Baseball was certainly going to miss him.

The second annual "Roanoke-Salem Baseball Hall of Fame" Hot Stove Banquet and Induction Ceremony took place on February 7th. Tug McGraw was the featured speaker, and the inductees were Baltimore Orioles manager Johnny Oates, who had played college baseball at Virginia Tech; former Mets catcher Ron Hodges, from nearby Rocky Mount, Virginia.; former Salem Rebels player and manager Jack Crosswhite; ex-major leaguer Russ Peters from Bedford, Virginia; and former Salem franchise owner Ralph Richardson.

We filled our job openings in February, hiring Ben Porter as groundskeeper and Stu Paul as our new play-by-play voice. Both had previous baseball experience, and we expected both to make an immediate contribution.

Less than a month after completing our staff, we lost a key member. Mike Baum's wife had accepted a new job on the other side of the state, and he reluctantly decided to make the move as well. The timing was bad, but he agreed to stay until the week before we opened the season. He had played a big part in producing our game program in '92 and would again be needed in that capacity. As we prepared to open the season, we would have little time to look for a replacement right away.

On April 12th, the day before our home opener, I encountered my first of what would amount to a number of differences of opinion with our groundskeeper. The entire staff was inside the park putting the finishing touches on everything in preparation for our first game the next day. Ben disappeared for several hours, and we were wondering what had happened to him.

Suddenly he showed up at the back gate and started cursing and threatening me because he had run out of gas while away from the park. He was saying it was my fault because I had not yet reimbursed him for several small receipts he had left on my desk. Maybe I'm behind the times, but if I don't have enough fuel to get to my destination I do something about it before undertaking my journey.

Regardless, we got into a heated exchange, and I informed him in no uncertain terms that I would not accept or tolerate this type of behavior ever again. If he had a problem, he could talk to me in a civilized manner or not at all! I would never talk to my superiors the way he was speaking to me.

*Jim "Catfish" Hunter and Sam at the seventh annual Old Timers' Game.*

That confrontation basically set the tone for our relationship from that point on. He said very little after that, instead doing whatever he felt needed to be done without consulting with anyone or getting clearance, even on stadium projects that required some type of pre-approval.

We opened the season with a six-game homestand that contained a little bit of everything from a weather standpoint, including sunshine, rain, high winds, and cool temperatures.

We won only two of the six games, but one went 14 innings before we won 12-11. We also dropped an exciting 11-inning contest, 7-6.

Timing is everything, and in late April we received a resumé from Anthony Marek. He had an impressive, well-rounded background, although no previous experience in baseball. We had not yet found time to hire a replacement for Mike Baum, and Anthony's credentials looked good. Dennis called him, he came to Salem to talk with us, we hired him, and he came on board in early May.

In our 23rd home game of the year on May 27th, we surpassed the 50,000 mark in season attendance, the earliest date in club history for reaching this goal.

As we moved into the month of June, the four teams in our division were battling for the top spot. On Friday June 4th, we were scheduled to play Frederick at home. That afternoon we caught a heavy thunderstorm and immediately put the tarp down. As five o'clock approached, the sky cleared and our staff headed over to the field to prepare for our game that night.

Just before we lined up to pull the tarp, the winds picked up and the sky began to look ugly. Greenish-black clouds appeared above the mountains on the horizon and began bearing down on us.

We decided to forget about the tarp and headed indoors, as the wind was now blowing harder than any we had ever experienced at the ballpark. Within minutes, the skies let loose with one of the worst storms imaginable. If it wasn't a small tornado, it was certainly close!

As we looked out the windows at the field, we saw the batting cage being blown across the diamond. In just a few more minutes, the rain became so hard and the sky so dark that we couldn't even see the ballpark!

The storm persisted for about a half hour, and we were forced to cancel our game that evening. Trees were uprooted all around the neighborhood, and power had been knocked out in many areas. Fortunately, our ballpark suffered only minor damage. Our Carolina League neighbor to the east, the Lynchburg Red Sox, weren't so lucky. Their park suffered extensive damage.

The following night we played a doubleheader to make up the postponement from the night before. Lynchburg was unable to make up their game because the repairs to their stadium would take a while to be completed.

Because of our proximity to Lynchburg, Paul Sunwall, their General Manager, called regarding playing a doubleheader at our park Sunday morning prior to our evening game. Because of the circumstances, we agreed to host their twin bill. As a result, we hosted our second triple-header in two seasons. Of course, this one was different in that our club wasn't playing all three games. Durham swept the doubleheader from Lynchburg, then we dropped a tough game to Frederick, 4-3, to complete the trifecta.

Also in early June, Pirates General Manager Ted Simmons suffered a heart attack and was rushed to a  hospital to undergo an emergency balloon angioplasty. Eleven days later Simmons resigned due to his health problems and Cam Bonifay was immediately named his successor.

I first met Bonifay in 1989 after he became the Pirates scouting director. He's a likeable, easy going, down-to-earth person. He has always been easy to talk to, and has always shown a great deal of concern for Pittsburgh's entire minor league system.

As the first half was winding down, our club tailed off, finishing at the bottom of our division with a record of 31-39. The Kinston Indians captured the crown in the South with a record of 38-31, three games in front of Durham. In the Northern Division, the new Wilmington Blue Rocks finished 9½ games ahead of runner-up Frederick, with the best record in the league at 44-25.

We moved into July and the heaviest promotional stretch of our season, with the San Diego Chicken on July 9th, followed the next night by our seventh annual "Old Timers' Game" featuring Catfish Hunter.

We also planned to resume our post-game concert series the following weekend. One of our local congressional delegates, Clifton "Chip" Woodrum, had introduced a bill changing the state law pertaining to the sale of beer during events connected with pro sports. Woodrum was instrumental in getting the necessary changes passed by the state legislature; without his assistance we would never have considered trying a concert again.

We also worked through a local concert promoter to put our show together, landing "Maurice Williams and The Zodiacs", along with "The Box Tops". We had learned our lesson with regard to working with outside promoters after our disastrous concert two years earlier.

The problems with our groundskeeper had persisted. I had several additional meetings with him, including one in which I had called him into my office for the sole purpose of firing him. Instead, wanting to be as fair as possible, I listened when he told me he would change his ways and try to communicate better. Unfortunately, any improvements were minor and short lived.

On Sunday July 11th, I arrived at my office at around 11 a.m. We had left the park late the night before because the "Old Timers' Game" had preceded our regular game, making it an exceptionally long evening. As I reached my desk, I found a note from Ben, worded in a threatening and derogatory manner regarding a $20 commission owed to him. It was the straw that broke the camel's back!

I was fed up with his unwillingness to work with me and my staff. If he had just talked with me about this situation he would have found that it had already been remedied. His check had arrived in our office on Saturday, but he had not come into the office to find out. Instead, he seemed to derive pleasure in trying to torment me and make my life difficult.

I went into the empty park and spotted him working near home plate. As I approached him from the grandstand, I told him I was tired of his disruptive behavior, fired him, and asked for his keys. He refused my request, then unleashed a verbal assault that would have curdled a sailor's blood. Dave Shonk had accompanied me into the park and at that point I asked him to call the police. After the police arrived, Porter became belligerent, had to be physically restrained, and ultimately was arrested and charged with disorderly conduct.

We were hoping that would be the end of it, but he then had a warrant issued against me, charging me with using abusive and threatening language. I would have to appear in court in August to answer his claims.

For the first time in club history, we surpassed the 100,000 mark in season attendance during the month of July. We did it on the night of our concert, July 17th.

At the end of the seventh inning during every home game, we brought soft drinks to the umpires on the field. This service was usually provided by our stadium waitresses who were known as Lady Bucs. One night in July, one of our concession workers, a high school student named Toby Rogers, offered to take the drinks out instead. Toby is a little on the heavy side and was wearing a pair of large shorts held up by a drawstring. As he approached home plate with a drink in each hand, the drawstring on his shorts came undone and his pants dropped around his knees. With a cup in each hand, Toby faced a dilemma. In front of a crowd roaring with laughter, Toby was the highlight of the evening as he juggled a soft drink in each hand while embarrassingly attempting to pull his pants back up. He finally succeeded, then, red faced, hurriedly disappeared back into the concession stand.

The Carolina League All-Star Game took place on Sunday, July 25th at Winston-Salem. We placed six players on the Southern squad, including pitchers Doug Harrah, Jason Christiansen, and Esteban Loaiza, along with catcher Angelo Encarnacion, third baseman Ken Bonifay, and first baseman/DH Mike Brown. Also named to the team were former Bucs Mariano De Los Santos, Jeff McCurry, and Tony Womack, but all three had been promoted to Carolina prior to the game.

The top power hitters in the league competed in a home-run-hitting contest prior to the game, with our Mike Brown winning the top prize of $100, in a tie-breaker with Doug Hecker of Lynchburg. Brown gave Hecker half the money.

On July 28th against the Frederick Keys, our club turned a triple play for the second time in two seasons. To turn a triple play two seasons in a row is unusual, but even more incredibly, both took place at home and both occurred on the same date, one year apart.

As July came to a close, our struggling ball club appeared headed for an eleventh consecutive losing half. Not since the first half pennant in '88 had our club finished above .500. Not very impressive. As we moved into the final month of the season, the only thing left to shoot for was another franchise attendance record.

Prior to our final road trip of the season to Wilmington, Delaware, and Frederick, Maryland, Scott Little requested that we line up a bus with a videocassette player to enable the team to watch movies during our longest trip of the season. He informed me that the players had agreed to pay the difference for a bus with a VCR. We made the arrangements and thought everyone was happy.

On the final day of that road trip our club was involved in a big brawl at Frederick after a pitch was thrown behind the head of one of our players, Joe Ronca. The team assumed this pitch was in retaliation for a beaning that had occurred the week before in Salem, when our pitcher, Dan Jones, hit Frederick's Basilio Ortiz in the head.

Ortiz had had to be assisted from the field and was taken to a local hospital, where he was diagnosed with a concussion. He missed several games as a result, and there was talk of getting even before the series in Frederick began.

Once that pitch soared behind Ronca's head, both dugouts emptied and the battle began. It was an all-out war, with Ronca and Frederick catcher Kris Gresham engaging in one of the main bouts, while Dan Jones was forced to fend off Ortiz and a number of other Frederick players.

When all the dust had settled and order was restored, we learned that the fight had started not because of the beaning, but because a former girlfriend of Ronca had dated Gresham the previous week when Frederick was in Salem. Because of the unusual twist, the story ended up on George Michael's "Sports Machine".

Shortly after the team returned from the road trip, several of the pitchers were running in the outfield before the next home game. They called me down to the field to talk with them. They began complaining about having to pay for a bus with air conditioning. I explained to them that the only thing they had been asked to pay for was a VCR that their manager had requested, and that our contract with the bus company called for all of our buses to be air conditioned. If they weren't, this was the first I had heard about it. They continued arguing with me, calling the ball club cheap and insisting that the extra money had gone toward getting a bus with air conditioning, rather than the VCR.

I offered to call the bus company to let them hear for themselves what they had paid for. Because it was close to game time, there were no takers, but several said they would stop by my office the following day to do so. I welcomed the opportunity to set the record straight.

In the meantime, a couple of the pitchers sat outside the clubhouse complaining about the situation to Ray Cox, the beat reporter from our local newspaper. Later that night, in the press box, he brought the complaints to my attention. I explained the situation to him, then called our bus company and handed him the phone. They confirmed the information I had given him. The only thing asked of the players, at their manager's request, was the extra payment for the VCR.

I thought that would be the end of it, and the following morning when nothing appeared in the paper, I let out a sigh of relief. My relief was short-lived, however. In Cox's Sunday baseball column, he wrote about the situation, including the comments by the players about the ball club being cheap. He had also quoted me as saying, "With the way our pitching staff has performed this season, if anyone has a right to complain it should be me." I had made the comment in jest after the incident and assumed it was off the record, as I make it a policy never to publicly criticize the performance of our players.

I apologized to our pitching coach, Dave Rajsich, about my comment having been printed. But I felt a total lack of class had been shown by the two pitchers, and they never made any attempt to apologize to the club for their remarks. All I can say is someday they'll grow up!

One of the requirements of the Professional Baseball Agreement was that minimum facility standards had to be met

*Municipal Field, Salem*

prior to April 1, 1994. The fact that we played in an existing facility made our requirements much less stringent than those relating to a new facility; nonetheless, some extensive renovations would be neededto meet the minimum requirements at Municipal Field.

Kelvin and I had met with Salem's Mayor, Jim Taliaferro, and Assistant City Manager Forest Jones after the '92 season to review those requirements. Both assured us that the necessary improvements would be made. The city then allocated $150,000 to meet the requirements.

Both Kelvin and I felt strongly that meeting the minimum standards was not necessarily in the best interest of the ball club. We felt our real need was a new stadium, because of the age of Municipal Field and its landlocked location. We simply couldn't make the modifications needed to allow us to operate profitably at that site. Despite all of our attendance records, the club had never shown a substantial profit, although we'd operate in the black.

We conveyed our feelings to the Mayor during our meeting, and he assured us that he would also like to see a new facility but was unable to give us a definite commitment as to when that might be possible. It was our feeling that if the city should spend $150,000 to improve Municipal Field, it would be even more difficult to convince City Council to spend the additional money required to build a new stadium.

In August we were notified that major league baseball was requesting a postponement by one year of any possible reopening of the Professional Baseball Agreement. Included in this request would be the postponement, also by one year, of the required stadium improvements. The request was approved by the minor leagues shortly thereafter, and we immediately informed the city of this new development.

We were able to convince the city to hold off on any major expenditures and to explore the possibility of building a new ballpark. They agreed to meet with us again at the end of the season to discuss these possibilities.

On August 20th, I went to court to answer the charges of using abusive and threatening language when firing our groundskeeper. The charges were dismissed, as Porter was unable to prove his claim, and the judge ruled that he had instigated his own termination by writing the derogatory note left on my desk.

Porter also filed for unemployment insurance, claiming he had been fired for an unjust cause. Because he had not worked long enough in Virginia, his claim was disallowed. He then filed an interstate claim through the Wisconsin labor board, where he had previously worked. After we filed a written report of the circumstances surrounding his dismissal, his benefits were denied by the state of Wisconsin.

He later appealed the decision, and we were involved in a telephone hearing in mid-October. Again, when all the evidence was presented, his claim was denied.

Over the years, finding a good public address announcer and a good team mascot have been almost as much fun as finding good groundskeepers. We've had some unusual characters in both positions.

One of the people who served as our "Rocky the Redbird" mascot had a habit of taking off the costume head while walking through the crowd. Despite the fact that the "Rocky" character was ugly, it was a tremendous improvement over his out-of-costume appearance. We had to demand that he keep the head on to avoid scaring the children.

Another of our more talented mascots would call in sick every time we were expecting a big crowd because of his fear of physical abuse from the youngsters in attendance. His value to the ballclub was greatly diminished by this phobia.

Jeff Dickerson, who served as our public address announcer for about six seasons, also developed a bad habit that we tried to break. For many years our radio broadcast booth was located on top of the stadium roof, while the press area containing the PA announcer and official scorer was located on a lower level. Despite our repeated demands for Jeff to stay at his position at all times, whenever there was a questionable scoring decision he would race to the roof to relay the scorers' call to the people in the radio booth.

One night as I watched Jeff sprint toward the roof, I had Brian Hoffman hide his microphone. When Jeff returned, he immediately panicked. I had disappeared before his return, and he had no idea that I was involved. He told everyone in the pressbox that if the mike wasn't returned pronto, he would inform me and heads would roll.

Of course, everyone in the pressbox knew I was involved and refused to tell him where the mike was hidden. They let him squirm for about a half inning before finally returning it, but by this time Jeff was in tears. I felt bad about making a grown man cry, but we were trying to teach him a lesson.

As we entered our final home series of the season on September 2nd, a surprise storm caught us off guard early in the day, dumping a great deal of water on the field before we managed to get the tarp down. We worked hard all afternoon to make the field playable, but neither manager wanted to play, partly because the game was meaningless since our opponent, Winston-Salem, had already qualified for the play-offs. They were hoping their team could rest and be ready for post-season play. Our club was hopelessly out of contention by this time, so our manager had no interest in playing either.

Both managers, Mark Berry of the Spirits and Scott Little, complained about the field conditions to the umpires. The field was playable. It wasn't perfect, but we had played under worse conditions many times in the past.

The campaigning by both managers was effective. We kept trying to persuade the umpires to start the game, but they continued to listen to the managers.

I finally called John Hopkins to inform him of what was going on. He was surprised that the umpires had not yet started the game and informed them that if we wanted to play, the field had better be in the worst condition either umpire had ever seen if they overruled us and postponed the game.

Both umpires agreed that the field certainly wasn't that bad but, against our wishes, they cancelled the contest anyway. We were upset, to say the least. We had spent all afternoon working to get the field ready, had dumped a number of bags of drying agents on the playing surface, and in the opinion of nearly everyone in the stadium, had made the field playable.

Unfortunately, in this case, the umpires had the final say and basically made a farce of the situation. The home plate umpire went out to the plate to accept the line-up cards wearing a t-shirt. Once the line-up cards were exchanged, the game was in his hands, and he called it off.

I called John Hopkins again to voice my concerns about the handling of the matter. After talking to a number of people at the park, he regretted not being more forceful with the umpires as it became clear that the managers had brow-beaten the umpires into cancelling the game. He vowed that changes in league policy would be instituted before the following season.

Several years earlier, we had experienced a similar situation, so we certainly hoped something would be done to prevent a repeat in the future. In fairness to the operators and fans, every game that can be played should be.

We ended the second half with a record of 30-40, in last place, nine games behind division-winning Winston-Salem. Frederick captured the top spot in the North, setting up first-round play-off matchups between Frederick and Wilmington in the North, and Kinston verses Winston-Salem in the South.

Wilmington struggled in the second half because a number of their players were promoted after they had won the first half crown. Off the field, however, their franchise was tremendously successful, leading the league in attendance for most of the season before finishing second to Frederick. Wilmington drew 332,132 in their first season after moving from Peninsula.

Frederick led the league, setting a new Class A record of 351,146. Durham finished third at 305,692. Despite our combined record of 61-79, worst in the league for the second year in a row, we drew 145,657 fans to set our seventh consecutive franchise record. We also extended our string of consecutive seasons of attendance growth to eleven, maintaining the longest streak in all of pro baseball.

Wilmington swept Frederick in round one of the play-offs, while Winston-Salem topped Kinston, two games to one. The Spirits then downed Wilmington, three games to one, to capture the league title.

Winston-Salem was led by Bubba Smith. Smith had almost singlehandedly carried the Peninsula offense in their championship season of '92 and started the '93 season at the Double-A level in the Seattle Mariners' organization. In late May, Smith was traded to the Cincinnati Reds' organization and assigned to Winston-Salem. In just 92 games, Smith connected for a league-leading 27 homers, knocked in 81 runs, led the league with a .585 slugging percentage, and became the first player in history to capture two consecutive Carolina League MVP Awards. Thanks in part to Smith, the Spirits also set a league home-run record with 160 for the season.

Felix Colon of Lynchburg was declared the league batting champ with a .320 average. Julian Tavarez of the Kinston Indians was voted top starting pitcher; he finished the season in the majors with the Cleveland Indians. Kinston's Dave Keller and Pete Mackanin of Frederick tied in voting for Manager of the Year, only the second time in league history the award had been shared. Vern Hoscheit of Greensboro and Pinky May of Burlington were co-winners in 1958.

None of our players made the end-of-season All-Star team, but Michael Brown put up some impressive numbers in capturing our team MVP award. He hit .271 with 25 doubles, 21 homers, 61 walks, 70 RBI, and a .486 slugging percentage. Ken Bonifay was having a tremendous year until a wrist injury pulled down his batting average, then ended his season in early August. He still managed to hit .277 with 18 home runs and 60 RBI.

*Two-time Carolina League MVP "Bubba" Smith led
Peninsula Pilots to the CL Championship in 1992 and
Winston-Salem Spirits in 1993.*

Our pitching staff finished last in the league in team pitching with a 4.43 ERA. One of the bright spots was Jeff McCurry, who broke the Salem single-season record for saves with 22, surpassing Joe Ausanio's 1989 total of 20 before being promoted to Carolina.

Tony Womack, our shortstop for the first half of the year, was promoted to Pittsburgh in September and saw some playing time in the big leagues.

Having lost a number of quality players to free agency in the two previous seasons, the Pirates struggled all year. Several more former Salem players received an opportunity to appear in the majors, including '92 Bucs Midre Cummings and Rich Aude. It was certainly a year of rebuilding, both for the Pirates, and for us. As we closed out the '93 campaign, a number of questions would have to be answered.

# 14 Where Do We Go From Here?

The first question we wanted answered was, "When can we expect a new stadium to be built?" Kelvin and I met again with Mayor Taliaferro and Forest Jones shortly after the conclusion of the '93 season to see if we could come up with a plan of attack and possible time frame.

The meeting was preceded by a meeting between myself, Forest Jones, and several of the city department heads in which we agreed that pumping money into Municipal Field was not a good idea because it was too old and would never meet all of the future requirements we expected major league baseball to demand.

We were also hearing grumbling from the Pirates about a new park. Their primary gripes revolved around the ballpark dimensions, complaining that their pitchers were being handicapped by our stadium. It seems they had forgotten how many of their current and former major league pitchers had pitched successfully in our park. Adapting to different ballparks is a part of player development.

Because the number of clubs is restricted by major league baseball and the N.A.P.B.L., many cities across the country have offered to build beautiful new stadiums to lure major league affiliations.

Even in the Carolina League, several new facilities were in use or being planned. Frederick was added to our league at the expense of Hagerstown, because of the prospect of a new stadium. The Peninsula team had been lured to Wilmington over the promise of a new, top-flight facility. Even the ever popular Durham Athletic Park was in the process of being eliminated because of plans for a beautiful new stadium in Durham.

Both Kinston and Winston-Salem had spent millions of dollars in upgrades to bring their stadiums in line with the new requirements. The only club in our league not needing major facility improvements was Prince William, but their stadium had been built within the past decade.

We agreed during our meeting with the Mayor that we would put together current figures on the economic impact we make in the community and would try to come up with some cost estimates on a new stadium, so the Mayor would have something to work with when he approached City Council to sell them on the idea. No definite commitment was made by the city and no specific time frame was established in which we could expect to see some action.

As we prepared for the '94 season, it appeared that our staff would remain intact. Our only real need would be another groundskeeper, although we also planned to create a new position.

We had seen tremendous growth in recent years in selling discounted season ticket books, as well as blocks of tickets for specific promotional events via telemarketing. We had subcontracted with outside firms to handle these sales, and had talked for several years about taking this operation "in house" to cut out the middle man and realize a larger profit. Our biggest problem was finding someone who could handle this job.

During the past season we had found that person. Glynn Greer had worked for us on a part-time basis, handling these responsibilities while working for an outside firm. He was a semi-retired local resident, interested in joining our staff on a permanent basis. In late February we brought him aboard as our new director of telemarketing.

We felt that we'd outgrown our old stadium. On nights when we had major events, parking was inadequate, the restroom facilities were inferior, and our concession set-up was archaic and inefficient. On medium-sized nights we were better suited to serve the customer.

By using telemarketing, we could spread out our crowds, strengthen our weaker nights, and break some of our bigger events up into a couple of nights. Thus we could operate a much more efficient stadium and increase our potential to turn a profit.

Telemarketing could also be utilized with a newer, more efficient stadium. You simply modify the way it is used to meet your new needs and increased capacities.

On October 21st we made the announcement that Trent Jewett would be our field manager in 1994. Jewett played in Salem as a backup catcher in '89, making him our second manager in a row to have spent time in Salem as a player. Jewett had spent '93 managing Augusta, where the team finished with an overall record of 59-82. Scott Little was reassigned to Augusta, basically flip-flopping assignments with Jewett.

Jewett ended his playing career at Carolina in '91 before being assigned to our club as a coach for the second half of that season. In '92 he managed Welland of the New York-Penn League in his managerial debut.

In late November, Mike Minshall, our former announcer, called to say that he had heard a rumor that Kelvin had agreed to sell the ballclub to a group headed by Eric Margenau, one of the former Peninsula owners. Margenau is currently part of a group owning the Capital City Bombers of the South Atlantic League and the Fort Wayne Wizards of the Midwest League.

We shrugged it off as a somewhat unlikely rumor, but since Minshall worked in the Midwest League, and his sources were probably the Fort Wayne people, there might have been some substance to it. We joked about it in the office before quickly dismissing it as just another rumor. However, deep down inside we had had some concerns that Kelvin might be trying to sell the team. Dennis and I had talked about it several times since the season ended, but each time would think of other reasons to justify the lack of interest we had detected in Kelvin in recent months.

We thought back to the negotiations over the new Professional Baseball Agreement prior to and during the Winter Meetings in Los Angeles in 1990. We knew Kelvin had lost a lot of his desire to own the team at that point, when the major leagues were successful in taking away a number of benefits and gained much greater control over their farm teams. We also knew Kelvin had received offers to sell the club over the years, and had been straightforward in saying that he would sell it for the right price. We took that to mean that he was not actively pursuing a sale, but would consider it if the right offer came along. He certainly didn't need the money, having been highly successful in the.Cable TV industry.

We headed off to the Winter Meetings in Atlanta on December 9th. Dennis and Dave rode with me during the seven-hour drive. My wife Sue, and Dennis's fiance, Anita, would drive down the following day to join us. Kelvin and his wife Jane had driven down a day earlier because Kelvin was to meet with Carolina League president John Hopkins to discuss some league business. This was not unusual, as Kelvin was one of the league vice presidents.

We met up with Kelvin that evening and went to dinner together. Afterwards, Kelvin asked me to come up to his room to look over some papers while Dennis and Dave decided to check out the social scene at our hotel.

When we sat down in Kelvin's room, he dropped the bombshell. He informed me that he had agreed to sell the club to a group headed by Eric Margenau. I told him about the phone call from Minshall and he was somewhat surprised that it had leaked out prematurely.

Kelvin explained his reasons for agreeing to sell, and I wasn't a bit surprised. He was concerned that no definite commitment to build a new stadium had been made by the city and felt that, without a new facility, the Pirates would probably not return to Salem after their current player development contract expired following the '94 season. The Pirates' pulling out wasn't the issue, as they had not done much to provide competitive clubs in recent years. But his feeling was that no other major league organization would be willing to replace them as long as we played in our old park.

Without a major league Player Development Contract, his current investment would be worth nothing. Even though he had not bought the team to make a lot of money, he didn't want to lose his investment completely. He had received a substantial offer, in the neighborhood of $2 million. Pretty hard to walk away from, considering the circumstances and possible alternatives.

His other concern was the fact that the Professional Baseball Agreement, although tabled for another year, was eventually going to be reopened. The general feeling around the minors was that the major league people were going to come after us again, this time for much more. With the state of the game on the big-league level, it only makes sense that the major leagues are going to continue looking for ways to cut costs and increase revenue.

As for my situation with regard to the sale, Kelvin assured me that the new ownership group was interested in keeping me with the club. In fact, Kelvin said that it was written into the bill of sale that the entire staff be retained, and he wouldn't have entered into the agreement under any other terms.

I was thankful for the opportunity to continue living and working in Salem, but I wasn't sure I wanted to work for this new group. What little I knew about the Peninsula operation involving Margenau was not good.

I didn't sleep well that night, for obvious reasons. The following day I attended several seminars with Dennis and Dave but kept quiet about the new developments, at Kelvin's request. At lunch with Kelvin that afternoon, we further discussed the situation. A number of people were already aware of the proceedings, and I informed Kelvin that I wanted to let Dennis and Dave know before they heard it from someone else. He agreed.

In the meantime, Kelvin and I met with Eric Margenau and several members of his group, and talked about the situation. Eric kept assuring me that he had no desire to make any changes, repeatedly stating that if something isn't broken, it doesn't need to be fixed.

After concluding our meeting, I headed up to my room to call Dennis and Dave to discuss the developments. We had a Carolina League 50th anniversary party scheduled for that evening, and it was already approaching the starting time of 5 p.m. Dennis was involved in setting up for this party and when I called his room and got no answer, I assumed he had already left for the gathering. He would have to be tracked down there.

My phone call woke Dave up. He had gone to his room to get a little rest and had fallen asleep. He said he was planning to go to the party soon, and I asked him to stop by my room first. In the meantime Sue arrived, and we discussed the latest developments. I had told her some of the details when we talked on the phone the night before, so she was already aware of much of what was transpiring.

Dave arrived at my room a short while later, and I let him in on what was going on. He was shaken by the developments but handled it well. We then headed down to the party and, once inside, immediately ran into Dennis. We asked him to come with us and left the room, finding a quiet location in the lobby where I informed him of the details of the sale. He took it much harder than Dave had, understandably so, as he was planning to get married in early January.

He understood the logic in the decision Kelvin had made, but probably best summed up the feelings we all had when he said, "I'm not totally surprised, yet, unlike with most other clubs, we always felt that as long as we did our jobs, we had a job." We were all aware that despite assurances to the contrary, this latest development could change that.

Two days later, on Sunday, I met again with Eric and his assistant, Jim Fargas. Also involved in our meeting were the general managers of Eric's other clubs, Bill Shanahan of Capital City and Mike Tatoian of Fort Wayne. I spent most of the meeting fielding questions that were being fired at me from all directions regarding our operation in Salem.

A number of positives were discussed relating to ways we could improve our current operation, but one thing was made perfectly clear. Without a new stadium, Eric would definitely move the club. He did say that if a new stadium were built in Salem, he had no intention of moving the team.

The following day, Monday, Kelvin called the city to inform them of the development, not wanting them to pick it up from a newspaper report. We had planned to meet with city officials as soon as we returned from Atlanta, but too many people were talking about the sale now. Kelvin spoke with

Forest Jones, who thanked Kelvin for calling and assured him that he would inform the Mayor.

We left Atlanta on Tuesday morning, returning to Salem. We were surprised that nothing had appeared in our local newspaper yet regarding the sale.

Over the weekend, Salem had played host to the NCAA Division III College Football Championship Game, "The Amos Alonzo Stagg Bowl". It had been a tremendous success and the city was basking in the glory. NCAA officials were ecstatic about the way Salem had presented itself in putting together a first-class event.

On Wednesday morning we held a staff meeting to discuss the situation and how to handle it when it became public knowledge. A short time later I received a call from Forest Jones informing us that a local newspaper reporter had just called the Mayor to ask some questions regarding the Stagg Bowl. He then asked the Mayor about future plans, including baseball. The Mayor assumed he already knew about the transaction and made a comment about it, catching the reporter totally by surprise. At that point the dam burst, and my phone began ringing off the hook.

We spent the remainder of the week dodging calls from radio and television stations, directing them to talk with Kelvin about the situation. We were not in a position to make any statements and had no intention of doing so.

Ray Cox, the baseball reporter for the *Roanoke Times*, was all over the story. Kelvin was not releasing too much information, sidestepping the issue as much as possible. The sale was not yet final and would not be until all paperwork was filed, then approval received from the Carolina League, the N.A.P.B.L., and major league baseball.

Cox wrote several articles about the proposed sale. His second, on Friday, December 17th, elaborated on the deficiencies of the current ballpark. He mentioned that the club could be forced to leave town or risk losing its pro baseball affiliation if a new facility wasn't built.

That may have been one of the most important articles ever written about baseball in Salem, because it effectively portrayed the seriousness of our predicament and the necessity of a new stadium if the desire to keep pro baseball in the Roanoke Valley really did exist.

It also prompted an onslaught of interest from local parties wanting to see a stadium built, as well as to buy the club to keep it in town. The article also fired up Mayor Taliaferro, pushing the new stadium possibilities to the forefront.

What also fired up the Mayor was a follow-up article detailing a plan by a sports-minded Roanoke City Councilman, Delvis "Mac" McCadden, a former pro umpire. Mac was interested in seeing a new facility built in downtown Roanoke to house the ballclub. The article disclosed that a private group had even gone so far as to hire HOK, an architectural firm well known in designing and building ballparks, to design a multi-purpose facility to be located in downtown Roanoke.

Salem takes tremendous pride in being a leader in the Roanoke Valley and in doing everything in a first-class manner. To think that the City of Roanoke might try to take away Salem's pro baseball team may have done more to fire up the Mayor than the thought of losing baseball altogether.

Regardless, Salem had become home to my family and me and the thought of the team being forced to leave because of an inadequate facility was not appealing. I've never worked with a city as cooperative. I've talked with many operators who, during my years in the game, were envious of the way we were treated by our city. I know of no other city that takes as much pride in the quality of life that it provides its citizens.

After the articles appeared in the paper, I visited Forest Jones and reiterated the points made in the newspaper regarding the facility. I also informed him of my conversation with Eric regarding the possiblity of the club being moved after the '94 season if a new facility wasn't built. I basically let him know that the threat was real!

On December 21st, I received the best Christmas present possible when Mayor Taliaferro called me at home at 7:30 that morning to tell me he thought he could get the necessary votes on council to get the stadium built. He also stated that if he did, there would definitely be strings attached, stipulating a long-term commitment to Salem by the ballclub, and possibly even a requirement of local ownership for the team.

I had no problem with these demands and felt that it only made sense for the city to protect itself if it were going to spend millions of dollars to build a new facility. The call was reassuring because I knew that Jim Taliaferro was the only person who could get a stadium built.

The Mayor sent a letter to John Hopkins, informing the Carolina League that Salem was in the process of securing funds for construction of a new baseball stadium to be ready by the spring of 1995. He also advised the league that Salem strongly objected to the sale of the Buccaneers to absentee owners as well as any attempt to move the club from the City of Salem.

I was mailed a copy of the letter and also noted that copies were sent to members of Roanoke City Council and the Roanoke County Board of Supervisors. I took this to signal that the Mayor was informing the other two local governments, as well as the Carolina League, that Salem was planning to fight to keep its team.

The December 30th issue of *The Salem Times-Register* had two major articles dealing with the developments. On the front page was a major story detailing the possibility of a new stadium. The article mentioned that Mayor Taliaferro had sent letters to officials of both Roanoke City and Roanoke County asking for financial support in the construction of the new facility. The bulk of the funding, and all costs relating to upkeep and maintenance, would be covered by Salem.

It appeared, according to the article, that the Mayor had the necessary votes on Salem City Council to get the plan approved.

Headlining the sports section was an editorial by Brian Hoffman that ranked right up there with Ray Cox's December 17th article in terms of importance to the cause. Brian elaborated on the benefits a new stadium would bring to the community. He also played up the "pride" aspect, so important to the City of Salem. He suggested the city should make the commitment because Salem always did things right, and a new ballpark would be keeping with that same tradition of excellence. It was a powerful editorial.

In mid-January, the major league owners met in Fort Lauderdale, Florida to try to resolve the appointment of a new commissioner. The owners had ordered their General Managers to stay away from the Winter Meetings in Atlanta, deciding to hold this separate meeting a month later instead.

No one understood the logic behind boycotting the Winter Meetings, but according to an article by Bob Nightengale in the December 13th *Baseball America*, California Angels General Manager Whitey Herzog said, "The owners wanted to try to protect themselves from spending so much money." The feeling was that if there were no Winter Meetings for the general managers, none of the teams would be able to get into bidding wars over free agents. Surprisingly, Herzog resigned his position with the Angels several weeks later.

The owners failed to elect a new commissioner during their meetings, when a majority of clubs refused to vote on the issue until a new collective bargaining agreement was in place to replace the one that had expired on December 31st. Attempts were being made to add a revenue-sharing plan and a salary cap to the new agreement, and the feeling was one of not wanting to add somebody new to the mix until this labor situation was resolved.

An agreement was reached with the Players Association on a new divisional alignment and play-off structure. They expanded from two to three divisions in each league, and added another tier to the play-offs by adding a wild-card team in each league along with the three division winners.

The sale of our club continued to be a hot topic in the media. A number of articles provided updates on the status of the sale. Everything was proceeding as expected, until it came time for the new owners to transfer the existing stadium lease. Without this lease, which would enable the club to play the 1994 season at Municipal Field, the prospective new owners would have little chance of the sale being approved by the Carolina League, as there were no alternative sites that fit within league confines.

On January 24th, the prospective new owners, Eric Margenau and Fred Mayerson, appeared before Salem City Council to request the lease be transferred to them. The city had not yet received all requested information relating to a background check on the new ownership group and decided to table the vote until the next council meeting on February 14th.

On February 13th, the third annual "Roanoke-Salem Baseball Hall of Fame" banquet and induction ceremony took place. The new inductees were Boyd Hall, an area coach and contributor to youth league baseball; Jack Dame, a former founder and General Manager of the Salem ballclub; and Charlie

Maxwell, the former major leaguer who won a Piedmont League triple crown while playing for the Roanoke Red Sox in 1949.

Also added were Bob Humphreys, the former big-league pitcher and current coordinator of player development for the Milwaukee Brewers, and Pablo Cruz, one of the most popular players ever to play professionally for Salem. Cruz was involved in that fatal collision in 1974 and talked about the tragedy earlier that day while visiting Municipal Field.

The following evening, Eric Margenau reappeared before Salem City Council to again request the transfer of the stadium lease. After much discussion, council decided that the issue of the lease transfer should be tied to discussion of a new ballpark, feeling that without the new stadium, there would be no baseball in Salem in the future, making the lease transfer a moot point. They tabled any action on the transfer until budget hearings scheduled in May.

Margenau was upset by this development. He argued that the two were separate issues, and warned that any further delay in the transfer of the lease could jeopardize the sale of the ballclub. Unfortunately for Eric, that appeared to be the intent of the city all along.

On February 28th, the expected date of the closing, the Carolina League informed Kelvin and Margenau that the sale would not be approved. As a result of the action taken by Salem City Council, the Carolina League Executive Committee recommended that the application for transfer of ownership be returned to Margenau.

The league, wary of possible litigation, rather than voting against the sale, instead voted not to approve it. The league felt that with the season approaching and no resolution expected until at least May, it was not in its best interest to approve the transfer of ownership.

In March, Salem City Council decided to let the issue of a new stadium be decided by the voters via a non-binding referendum to be held on July 19th.

As the '94 season approached, the big story in the minor leagues was Michael Jordan. Jordan had retired from the NBA in the fall of '93 after leading the Chicago Bulls to their third straight NBA title, and he decided to give pro baseball a try. He had signed with the Chicago White Sox organization but struggled during spring training and there was some talk that he might start the season at Prince William in the Carolina League. We were already receiving calls and by late March, had sold over 100 tickets for their first scheduled visit to Salem on May 2nd. Instead, Jordan was assigned to the Birmingham Barons of the Double-A Southern League, with plans to move him along quickly to Triple-A Nashville, then to the majors.

Despite finishing the first half with a record of 32-37, our 12th straight losing half, we stayed in the pennant chase until the end. The entire Southern Division played below .500 for most of the half, with Winston-Salem finishing on top with a record of 35-33. Wilmington ran away with the Northern Division, posting the best record in the league at 48-20.

The Carolina League All-Star Game was scheduled for July 20th in Wilmington. On July 19th, the date of the stadium referendum, we headed to Wilmington for the All-Star Game festivities, which included a banquet that evening. During the banquet, Kelvin placed a call to the Roanoke Valley to get the referendum results. The new stadium had been approved by a whopping 85 percent of the voters, an extremely high margin for a vote of this type. We would finally be getting our new stadium.

We placed eight players on the Southern Division All-Star team: catcher Jason Kendall, third baseman Jay Cranford, second baseman Chance Sanford, designated hitter Danny

Clyburn, and pitchers Sean Evans, Marc Wilkens, Sean Lawrence, and Marc Pisciotta. Pisciotta had been leading the league in saves before being promoted to Carolina several weeks earlier and was unavailable for the game.

In a spectacularly staged All-Star event, the North beat the South on a dramatic home run in the bottom of the ninth by Wilmington catcher Lance Jennings.

During the season the Prince William Cannons had a back-up catcher named Jack Johnson who became somewhat of a celebrity, hosting his own radio show. "Bullpen Chat" provided a humorous look at the game as seen from the bullpen. During the Cannons final trip into Salem in mid-August, he put on our groundskeepers goggles, tarp boots, tarp gloves, and overalls, then warmed up a pitcher in the bullpen.

Later, when starting catcher Robert Machado was injured in a collision at the plate, the call went out for Johnson. He was nowhere to be found. Eventually he was tracked down in our groundskeepers shed, watching "Ghostbusters II" on television. He reluctantly pulled himself away from the movie and entered the game.

On August 12th, the major league players went on strike due to the impasse in contract negotiations with the owners. The last major walkout by the players had occurred during the 1981 season and had lasted 50 days, leading to a boom in minor league baseball. The current strike was expected to have the same effect, but because the minor league season ends around Labor Day, we would have only a little more than three weeks to benefit from being "the only game in town."

The combination of the strike, beautiful late-season weather, and the hype surrounding the closing of our old ballpark enabled us to overcome another lackluster perfor-mance on the field. The fans again came out in record numbers, as we set our eighth consecutive franchise attendance record and extended our streak of consecutive years of attendance growth to 12. A crowd of 5,467 in what we thought would be our final game ever at Municipal Field pushed our season total to 153,575.

A better script could not have been written for the finale, as Reed Secrist hit a pinch-hit three-run homer in the bottom of the eighth to carry us to a 7-6 win over Lynchburg. Ironically, the first pro game ever played at Municipal Field, on May 20, 1939, also saw Salem top Lynchburg.

Unfortunately, we also extended our string of consecutive losing halves to 13, finishing the second half at 32-38. Durham won the second half in the South but fell to first half-winning Winston-Salem in the first round of the play-offs. Wilmington closed strongly to finish on top again in the North, then swept Winston-Salem in the finals to capture the league title.

Wilmington also dominated post-season honors, with Mike Jirschele being named manager of the year, first baseman Larry Sutton capturing the MVP award, and Bart Evans being named pitcher of the year. Center fielder Johnny Damon and designated hitter Andy Stewart were also named to the year-end all-star team. Sutton had an outstanding season, posting a .306 average, with 26 homers and 94 RBI.

Our lone representative on the post-season squad was Chance Sanford, the utility infielder. Our top performer all season had been catcher Jason Kendall, who finished second in the league with a .318 average, 7 homers and 66 RBI.

On September 14th, the remainder of the major league baseball season, along with post-season play, was called off by acting commissioner Bud Selig due to a lack of progress in resolving the strike. The following day, we held a news conference to announce the signing of a new four-year player development contract with the Colorado Rockies, terminating our long relationship with the Pirates.

*Certificate of attendance for what we thought would be our last game in Municipal Field.*

In mid-November, we unveiled our new logo and nickname, becoming the Salem Avalanche. We also adopted the purple, silver, and black colors worn by the Rockies.

Despite possibly being the greatest basketball player of all time, Michael Jordan continued to struggle with baseball. After spending the entire season at Birmingham, hitting just .202 with 3 homers and 51 RBI in 127 games, Jordan played in the fall Arizona Instructional League where he showed some improvement. But in mid-March, Jordan gave up his attempt to reach the major leagues and returned to pro basketball. Many had felt that Jordan's superb athletic prowess would lead to his quick ascension to the majors, but instead, the difficulties encountered by Jordan emphasized how tough playing professional baseball really is.

*Construction of Salem Memorial Baseball Stadium.*

# 15 Hurry Up And Wait

A year of change, a new nickname, new logo, and eventually a new stadium. Four additional front office people at last gave us enough people to cover all key areas. We were finally able to departmentalize, with a Ticket Manager, Director of Merchandising, and Director of Group Sales, to go along with what we already had. Each department head was able to hire additional people to staff their department.

My wife Sue had taken on the full-time position of Director of Merchandising. She had handled our souvenir department in the past, but with the new nickname and logo, our souvenir sales exploded.

In anticipation of the new stadium, we added Mike Holdren as our Director of Ticket Operations. He had been a ticketing assistant in Wilmington the previous season. It was imperative that we upgrade our ticket operations at the new ballpark.

Deron Marchant was hired as our new Director of Group Sales. He had spent the previous season with the Oklahoma City '89ers and had worked in the Carolina League in Winston-Salem several seasons earlier.

Anthony Marek left the club to take a radio position with the Lynchburg Hillcats, joining many of our former Salem Buccaneer players. Pittsburgh became affiliated with the Lynchburg club after the Red Sox decided to leave the Carolina League and we affiliated with the Rockies. Marek was replaced by Lara Steward, who became our new Director of Community Relations.

We also decided to change radio announcers, letting Stu Paul go at the end of the '94 season and replacing him with Mark Neely prior to the start of the new season. Neely had been the number-two announcer at Triple-A Louisville for the past three years.

Unfortunately, the most important part of the equation, the new stadium, took the longest to materialize. As the winter months elapsed, the stadium slowly began to take shape. We had spent the entire off-season selling advertising and tickets on the premise of being in the new stadium by opening day.

As April rolled around, it became apparent that we would not achieve our goal. The stadium was still a long way from completion. We hoped that by early May we could be in the new stadium, but it still wasn't ready.

June 20th, the start of the second half, was the next date that the contractors had assured us of being in the park. In fact, they had even gone so far as to guarantee that we would be in there by the preceding Friday, June 16th.

But June came and went and still no ballpark. In the meantime, we continued to play at Municipal Field. We had done very little to upgrade Municipal because we were under the impression from day one that if we did indeed play there, it would be on a very temporary basis. As the days turned into weeks, then months, we became more and more frustrated.

We had hired many additional stadium employees prior to the start of the season, but when we opened at the old park, we were unable to use all of them. We tried to rotate them to keep everyone working, but many were unhappy with the number of hours they were getting and left for other jobs.

We had also increased our billboard advertising from 38 signs in the old park to 52 in the new. Our sign painter had a crew working round the clock all winter long to be sure all 52 signs would be in place by the original April 14th deadline. We had absorbed a great deal of additional costs to be sure that all our deadlines were met.

When it became apparent that we would open in the old park, it was too late to accommodate our advertisers. All the signs were already painted and in place in the new park.

On July 14th, we closed a home series against Lynchburg. We'd had a number of bus problems over the years, and the Lynchburg club uses the same bus company. About two hours before game time, Marc Hill, the Lynchburg manager, called to say that their bus had broken down several miles from the ballpark. We hopped into our vehicles and provided a shuttle service for the Lynchburg players.

We had owned Lynchburg nearly all season and had beaten up on them pretty good the two previous nights. Several of their players joked about us making sure we got them to the park so we could beat up on them again. Unfortunately, as is usually the case in similar circumstances, they turned the tables on us that night.

Speaking of beating up on someone, on May 22nd, our first home game against Lynchburg earlier in the season, we had just broken the game open with a big rally in the bottom of the 7th. Our catcher, Randy Snyder, was tagged out at the plate by pitcher Jason Pfaff while trying to score on a wild pitch. Pfaff appeared to rub the ball in Snyder's face as he slid head first and Snyder came up swinging. Both benches emptied, but the situation amounted to just some minor pushing and shoving.

Both Snyder and Pfaff were ejected from the game. Also, upon reading the umpires' report, President Hopkins issued nearly $4,000 in fines and about 80 games in suspensions, adhering to the new anti-violence rules enacted by the minor leagues. The minimum penalty for anyone leaving the bench or their position during an altercation is a $100 fine and a two-game suspension.

Our skirmish was minor in comparison to what went on to our south at the same time. In a brawl that was shown on ESPN, CNN, and many other major network newscasts, the Durham Bulls and Winston-Salem Warthogs saw $6,100 levied in fines and 122 games in suspensions on "Strike Out Domestic Violence" Night in Durham.

Warthogs pitcher Glen Cullop had his jaw broken and lost four teeth when Bulls relief pitcher Earl Nelson kicked him in the face. Nelson received the strongest penalty, six games. When his suspension ended on May 31st, he was released by the Atlanta Braves.

July 25th became the next target date to move into the new stadium, officially our third. We all felt that the date would be attainable because the stadium was beginning to look like one of the finest minor league parks in the country. However, safety rails and concession ductwork were not finished by the target date and again we were left playing at Municipal Field.

By now many were thinking that we would not get into the new park all season, but, even worse, some thought we'd been aware of this from day one and had deceived the public. But intentionally misleading anyone on this issue would have served no purpose. If we had known all along we wouldn't be in the new park, we would have handled our advertising differently. We were losing a great deal of money every day by not being in the new stadium.

The next scheduled homestand was to start on August 7th. Things were coming together nicely now and, despite the cries of some fans to wait until next year to open the new park, we were intent on saving face by getting in as soon as possible.

On August 1st it became official. We held a news conference to announce that we would open the new "Salem Memorial Baseball Stadium" on August 7th. Tickets went on sale the following day at the new stadium box office, and we sold out

*Colorado Rockies Mascot "Dinger the Dinosaur" stopped by Municipal Field to sit on Avalanche pitcher Doug Million; Vinnie Garcia and pitching coach Billy Champion look on.*

the 6,000-seat stadium officially on August 5th. We continued to sell standing-room-only tickets and opened the park with an official paid attendance of 6,421.

Appropriately enough, it seemed that first game would take nearly as long to play as it had taken the stadium to be built. We finally won on a bases-loaded walk to Forry Wells in the bottom of the fifteenth inning, 3-2 over Frederick.

Doug Million started the game and threw the first pitch in the new stadium, a strike. The first hit was a single in the bottom of the first by our second baseman, Vincente Garcia.

Despite the fact that the stadium was not 100-percent complete, we were finally in it! It still lacked some of the safety rails, two staircases located at the ends of the grandstands, two concession stands, our souvenir store, and administrative offices. Regardless, knowledgeable people were proclaiming it one of the finest minor league parks in the country.

It features twelve luxury skyboxes, three complete club-houses (an extra for tournaments and special events), an extremely large and well-equipped press box, spectator decks, a state-of-the-art sound system, and scoreboard with full-color animations and replay capability.

All summer long our attendance had been negatively influenced by both the prolonged wait to enter the new stadium (many of our regular fans refused to come out to Municipal Field while awaiting the grand opening), and the continued major league problems.

The major league owners had declared an impasse in negotiations and invoked a salary cap. The players refused to report. The major league clubs then hired replacement players, primarily recently retired or released players, along with un-signed free agents from some of the independent clubs, and minor leaguers.

On March 31st, just two days before the major league season was set to begin with the replacement rosters, the players' association was granted an injunction restoring the previously existing labor rules. The owners then agreed to reinstate the previous guidelines in lieu of a settlement and halted the start of the replacement season. This sent the regular big leaguers to the training camps, causing the major league season to start on April 25th with an agreed upon shortened schedule.

With no play-offs or World Series in 1994, and apparently no definitive solution to the labor dispute, many fans had become disenchanted with professional baseball. Even after the major league season resumed, attendance was down dramati-

*The unveiling of the Salem "Sports Nut" on August 7th, 1995, as Salem Memorial Baseball Stadium opens. From left: Salem Councilman Alex Brown, 6th District Congressman Bob Goodlatte, Carolina League President John Hopkins, Salem Mayor Jim Taliaferro, and the Nut.*

cally at most ballparks. Some of the minor league clubs were feeling the effects also.

The combination of fan apathy toward pro baseball, and our inability to get into our new stadium until August 7th, brought about an end to our streak of twelve consecutive years of attendance growth. Despite an average attendance of nearly 3,500 per game in the new park, it was too little, too late. Had we gotten in one homestand earlier, we probably would have kept our streak alive.

Fortunately for major league baseball, 1995 was the year of the streak. Cal Ripken, Jr.'s streak that is. On September 6th at Camden Yards, Ripken played in his 2,131st consecutive game, eclipsing the long-thought-unbreakable record held by Lou

Gehrig. With a build-up reminiscent of Henry Aaron chasing Babe Ruth's all-time home run record, or Pete Rose's quest of Ty Cobb's career hits mark, the eyes of the world were focused on Ripken, as he handled the pressures leading up to the incredible accomplishment with dignity. The class shown by Ripken throughout his quest did wonders in bringing popularity back to the game.

What was even more incredible about Ripken's streak is that he also played in over 99 percent of the innings during the streak, and most at the demanding shortstop position. When the streak began, Reggie Jackson, Johnny Bench, Willie Stargell, Rod Carew, and Carl Yastrzemski were all still playing.

Speaking of playing, one of our nightly features is an on-field promotion at the end of the fifth inning called the "dizzy bat race". Two contestants are chosen to go on to the field, place their heads on a bat, spin around ten times, then race to first base.

One night shortly after moving into the new stadium, our two contestants were elderly ladies. One of them lost her balance, and when an usher tried to keep her from falling, she went head over heels, taking the usher down underneath her. It was the highlight of the night as the fans roared.

Fortunately, no one was hurt, but I held my breath throughout, sensing a lawsuit just waiting to happen.

Speaking of lawsuits, 1995 was the year that you needed a scorecard to keep track of all we were involved in. The first stemmed from a youngster who had been hit by a foul ball during the 1992 season. Despite the fact that you enter a ballpark at your own risk, his lawyers smelled a big payday.

The second incident involved a break-in by one of our employees. He was a high school football star looking for summer work before entering college on a football scholarship. The incident took place early in the season while we were still at Municipal Field. Despite his theft of over $1,000 and a high-speed auto chase resulting in what could have been a serious accident, he was let off virtually free.

The third involved Anthony Marek, our former employee. He brought suit against the club, claiming he was owed sales commissions even though we'd been obligated to refund advertising money when we were unable to get into the new stadium until August 7th.

We were threatened with another lawsuit by a woman claiming to have been run over in our stadium by a youngster during a post-game concert. We were unable to find anyone who had witnessed this incident.

The latest lawsuit stemmed from the relocation of the NHL's Quebec Nordiques to Denver, where they became the Colorado Avalanche. It was our contention that we owned the rights to the Avalanche nickname, having conducted an exhaustive search, then trademarking and registering the name. What good are copyright laws if they don't mean anything?

Our first year of affiliation with the Rockies was a welcome change. The players came to Salem with a much better attitude than many of the recent teams sent by the Pirates, despite playing much of the season at Municipal Field.

The first half was one of many short winning and losing streaks. Consistency was a problem, especially from our bullpen. It was our lack of a solid pen that kept us from seriously contending all season.

On June 2nd, we were rained out of our game with Prince William. The rain was falling steadily right through game time, leaving us no option but to keep the tarp down and schedule a doubleheader the following evening.

Apparently, several players decided they'd like to have the following night off also, returned to the stadium late at night, and attempted to remove the tarp. They were only partially successful, perhaps underestimating the weight of the water on the tarp. They managed to uncover about half the infield, and the heavy overnight rain made quite a mess.

Fortunately, the sun came out the next morning, and our ground crew worked all day to put the field back together.

We stayed in the pennant race for most of each half but, unfortunately for us, the strongest team in the league, the Kinston Indians, were in our division. They caught fire in May and June and ran away from the rest of the league.

We placed four players on the mid-season Southern Division All-Star team: pitcher Jamey Wright, shortstop Chris Sexton, and outfielders Brian Culp and Edgard Valasquez.

The All-Star Game was played in Lynchburg and was won by the Northern Division squad, 8-3.

In the second half, Kinston slumped somewhat, losing several key players to injuries, including Pitcher of the Year Bartolo Colon. They still had enough to win the second half crown as well, then swept Northern Division Champion Wilmington in three straight in the final series. Wilmington had won the second half in the north, then swept first-half winner Prince William in two in the only semi-final series.

Kinston first baseman Richie Sexson was named Player of the Year on the basis of his .306 average, 22 homers, and 85 RBI. Wilmington catcher Mike Sweeney led the league with a .310 average, was named to the year-end All-Star team, and was promoted to the big leagues when Kansas City called him up before the final play-off series.

Wilmington manager John Mizerock was named skipper of the year in guiding the Blue Rocks to the best overall record by virtue of a 48-21 second half. Our center fielder, Edgard Velasquez, led our team with a .300 average. He finished third in the league behind Sweeney and Sexson, and was our lone representative on the year-end All-Star team.

*Avalanche pitcher Jamey Wright bringing the heat. Wright was the first from our Rockies affiliation to make "The Show."*

Despite the improved attitude from the Rockies farm hands, the string of consecutive losing half seasons continued. We finished both halves with identical records of 34-36 for an overall mark of 68-72, extending our string to 15 consecutive losing halves.

All of the publicity surrounding the delays, and the hype over the opening of the new stadium, led to a tremendous increase in fan awareness. The term "being in a fish bowl" took on a whole new meaning for me and my staff. Everything we did was magnified by media coverage and crowds much larger than we were accustomed to.

We welcomed and appreciated most of the scrutiny, but it didn't take long to realize that nearly everyone has an opinion of how they can do your job better than you can. More importantly, they all want to prove it.

# 16 Opting For Free Agency

Kelvin made it clear that now that we were finally in the new stadium, he would take a more active role in the operation. Earlier in the season, he started looking for an additional strong front-office person to help with our increased sales load, as well as with some of the enormous operations responsibilities required by the new facility. By the time the season ended, however, his plans had changed considerably.

On September 28th, he told me that he had finally found the person we were looking for. He also said that the only way we could get him to come would be to make him General Manager and give him much of the day-to-day operational responsibilities. My biggest concern was how my role would change and what duties I would retain.

Kelvin portrayed it as a promotion for me. I would be named Executive Vice President of Business Operations and would handle many of the accounting chores that I was already involved in. I was not pleased with my diminished role in the day-to-day operation and expressed this concern to Kelvin. It was my feeling that we needed more Indians, not another chief! Kelvin did not agree and a heated debate followed. Ultimately, it was his team and he could do whatever he wanted.

At the conclusion of our meeting, Kelvin assured me that he would do nothing without my blessing. All details would be worked out to everyone's satisfaction before the position was even offered. He also indicated that I would continue to have much to say regarding operations, and he looked forward to my working for him for another ten years.

For some reason I wasn't buying into it. I'd begun to see a different side of Kelvin and was no longer comfortable with where he was coming from. Recently he'd been making derogatory remarks about me to media people behind my back, as if to show them he was in charge. I never questioned his authority, but I believe he resented, and may have felt threatened by all the credit I was receiving for the success of the franchise. He was definitely not the same person that I had come to work for ten years earlier. Others who had known him for a while were saying the same thing.

Nothing more was said regarding a new General Manager until several weeks later when Sue called one of our suppliers to place a cap order. She was told that Dave Oster, an assistant General Manager with the Wilmington Blue Rocks, was coming in to run the entire show. Later that day we received a similar call from one of the teams in our league. So much for everything being worked out to everyone's satisfaction beforehand.

Later that day I questioned Kelvin about the reports, and he denied that anyone had been offered the position, let alone agreed to take the job. Several days later he called to say that Oster was planning to join us on November 1st, and he set up a conference call among the three of us.

Oster began work on November 1st, but even then no clear definition of roles and responsibilities was presented. Despite the way the situation was handled, it still could have worked if all of us had known what was expected of us.

I continued to press Kelvin for a set of job descriptions, and he assured me that he was working on them. He finally presented them to the staff in early January. I had been expecting the worst, and I wasn't disappointed. It was as if Kelvin had created two separate offices.

My responsibilities included running the sales operation, along with all accounting duties. I was to answer directly to Kelvin, as always, but I had no authority over anyone in the office. All staff members were to answer to Oster. The normal progression would have been for Oster to answer to me but, instead, Oster also was to answer to Kelvin.

Despite the two-headed dragon that had been created, we continued to move forward in anticipation of our first full season in the new stadium. After hearing tales of continuous sell-outs in Wilmington, Kelvin decided that we should raise our season ticket prices and do away with our popular discounted ticket books.

We hired five interns at the Winter Meetings in Los Angeles and added them to our in-house telemarketing operation in January. Despite the increased manpower, our telemarketing operation was a disappointment. We entered the season having sold considerably fewer season tickets than in the previous year.

Stadium construction was still being completed as we approached the season. A large picnic area was finished prior to opening night, and on May 31st, a monument constructed near the stadium entrance was dedicated to area war veterans. It wasn't until August 2nd that we opened our stadium souvenir store, and mid-October before we finally moved into our new administration building.

One outstanding addition to the new stadium stemmed from a promotion sold by our Director of Stadium Operations, Stan Macko. A hot tub was installed by a sponsor, enabling us to rent it out on a nightly basis. A group of six to ten people could watch the game from its location down the right field line, just past the grandstand. We had nearly sold a similar promotion in

1992, but serious physical limitations in our old ballpark prevented us from carrying it out.

The hot tub brought us some tremendous national and even international exposure. It was mentioned in *USA Today Baseball Weekly*, which led to an article in the *Washington Post*. ABC's *Good Morning America* then picked up the story, followed by *CBS This Morning* with a live report from the tub itself. The E! Entertainment cable network showed clips from the CBS report on its *Talk Soup* program. Even the Japanese Fuji TV network sent a film crew to Salem to cover the event.

On the field our string of ineptitude continued. We got off to a fast start and led our division during the early part of the season, but an extended losing streak dropped us to 34-35 at the end of the half. We finished only four games out of first, but were last in our division.

We had not finished above .500 since the first half of the 1988 season, the last season Bob Teitlebaum had covered the team regularly. The curse of Teets continued in the second half, as we were never in contention, finishing at 28-41. Our streak of consecutive losing halves had been extended to 17.

The major league season had gotten off to an inauspicious start with the comments of Marge Schott again shooting baseball in the foot. Following two strike-plagued seasons, the last thing the game needed was an owner publicly extolling the virtues of Adolph Hitler. Schott received a three-year suspension from day-to-day operations in Cincinnati, much to the delight of the Reds' front office.

We hosted the Division III College Baseball World Series in late May, putting our team on the road for ten days. The club returned to open a homestand on May 31st against Frederick with pitcher Luther Hackman on the mound. Hackman was struggling early in the game when Eric Chavez lined a fastball off Hackman's face. The ball rolled to first baseman John

*The internationally renowned hot tub at
Salem Memorial Baseball Stadium.*

Fantauzzi, who recorded the putout before racing to the mound to assist Hackman. Hackman was unconscious, suffering from a broken nose, broken cheekbone, and concussion. Blood was pouring from his face, and he was removed from the field by ambulance and rushed to a local hospital. Hackman began a slow recovery, missing over a month before taking the mound again.

On June 16th, the Carolina Leage All-Star Team flew to California to take on the California League All-Stars at Rancho Cucamonga, in the first ever coast-to-coast meeting of two Class A leagues. Shortstop Kyle Houser and pitcher Doug Million represented Salem in the contest that ended controversially in a 2-2 deadlock, when Cal League Manager Del Crandall refused to continue after 11 innings because he had run out of pitchers. In fact, utility infielder Joe Urso received a standing ovation when he pitched the 11th inning for the Cal League and retired the side in order.

No one was happy with the tie, especially Carolina League Manager Jack Mull (Kinston) and league president John Hopkins. Both felt the game should have been played to a conclusion and blamed the Cal League for not having enough pitchers. Even Cal League President Joe Gagliardi felt the game should have continued. Had he not interceded, Crandall would have quit after the tenth inning. Regardless, both leagues agreed that rules regarding extra innings would be more clearly defined before the '97 meeting in Durham.

In early July, pitcher Jamey Wright made his major league debut for the Rockies againt San Francisco in a game televised on ESPN. Wright had been the ace of our staff in '95 and started the season at Double-A New Haven before an early promotion to Triple-A Colorado Springs. Wright picked up the win with an effective performance, completing his journey from Class A to the major leagues in less than one year. Wright remained in the Rockies rotation for the remainder of the season, posting a winning record and at times looking brilliant.

The new stadium was responsible for some player activity that would never have happened at our old place. Second baseman Eric Young was assigned to Salem on injury rehabilitation early in the year. Young returned to the Rockies shortly thereafter and was named to the National League All-Star Team in July. He also contended for the NL batting title for much of the season before tailing off late. He led the NL in stolen bases with 53.

Pitcher David Nied, the first player selected by the Rockies in the expansion draft, was also assigned to Salem in July after struggling at Triple-A. Nied settled down and pitched extremely well at times, and was recalled by the Rockies in September.

On August 7th, Larry Walker arrived to begin his comeback from a broken collarbone. He played two game for us and went four for eight with three doubles and a towering home run off the scoreboard in right center field. Most impressive was how hard he played the game, despite just coming back from a serious injury. He opened the eyes of many who expected him

*Pitcher Luther Hackman felled by a line drive
on May 31, 1996 at Memorial Stadium.*

to do little more than show up. Upon returning to Colorado, he hit two homers in his first three games back.

Bill Swift also made several starts for us in August before his recall to Colorado. Swift was recovering from major arm surgery and struggled at times in Salem but did pick up a win and a save right after returning to the Rockies.

Salem played in another tripleheader on August 1st, this time at Frederick. The Keys won the completion of a suspended game, followed by another victory in the second game. The Avalanche came from a 4-1 deficit in the final inning to tie, then win with five in the top of the 11th of the final contest. The suspended game was resumed at 3:30 and the final game concluded at 11:30, providing a day of baseball that even Ernie Banks might have grown tired of.

Luther Hackman was on the mound in Salem on August 4th as the Avalanche hosted Kinston. After walking two and hitting a batter in the first inning to load the bases, pitching coach Billy Champion visited the mound and verbally tore into

Hackman. Whatever he said worked, as Hackman pitched out of the jam after allowing a run. At one point he retired 16 in a row in hurling the first no-hitter in Salem Memorial Stadium history. The Avalanche won, 4-1, marking an incredible comeback by Hackman after his devastating injury in May.

The lawsuits that had begun a year earlier were resolved, but not all to our liking. Anthony Marek was awarded the commission money he had requested, despite credits and refunds due on the accounts in question. The figures were adjusted downward to accurately reflect the actual amount that he hadn't received.

The suit being brought on behalf of the youngster hit by a foul ball was settled out of court, with the insurance company agreeing primarily to cover medical bills. Only the attorneys made anything additional on this, as it had been dragged out for several years despite the fact that proving the ballclub negligent would have been difficult.

Our trademark dispute with the Colorado Avalanche was brushed aside as Kelvin decided that protecting our trademark would probably not be worth the expense, considering the uncertainty of a court ruling.

During the early part of our season Dave Oster began seeing a woman who had been working as a sales representative for a local radio station. Her name was Lisa Aliff, and she was a former Miss Virginia. She had also been an actress, appearing on "Cheers" and in the movie "Dragnet", starring Dan Aykroyd. A Roanoke Valley native, she and her former husband, a local businessman, were involved in a custody dispute over their six-year-old son. The dispute centered around an alleged affair between Aliff and Aykroyd which Aykroyd had vehemently denied. During testimony in the custody trial, Aliff admitted to having a "relationship" with

Aykroyd, prompting the actor and his spokespeople to refuse any additional comments.

As the season progressed, Oster's relationship with Aliff heated up, despite the fact that Oster also had a serious relationship with another woman who lived out of town. Every few weeks the out-of-town girlfriend would arrive for a visit and the entire staff would delight in the juggling act performed by Oster.

Oster was successful in keeping the two apart until July, when Aliff decided to bring the matter to a head by confronting the other woman in the ballpark during a game. She never got the opportunity. She was removed from the stadium beforehand, and at that point Oster broke off their relationship despite numerous attempts by Aliff over the next few weeks to change his mind.

Wilmington and Durham were division winners in the first half, but immediately following the All-Star game in California, four members of the Bulls were promoted to Double-A, including outfielder Andruw Jones. Jones was hitting .313 with 17 homers, 43 RBI, and 16 stolen bases at the midway point. He went on to hit .369 at Greenville, then .378 at Triple-A Richmond with a combined minor league total of 34 home runs, 92 RBI, and 30 stolen bases before joining the Atlanta Braves in just his second pro season.

At the age of 19, Jones became the youngest player in major league history to hit post season and World Series home runs. He was named minor league Player of the Year for the second consecutive season by *Baseball America*, joining Greg Jefferies as the only other two-time winner.

Without Jones, Durham tailed off in the second half, finishing third behind Southern Division-winning Kinston. Wilmington again finished first in the North to lock up a spot in the finals while awaiting the winner of the first round series between Kinston and Durham.

Kinston won the first game at home, but Hurricane Fran ripped through the region the following day, devastating the Kinston ballpark and knocking out power in the Durham area for several days. The clubs traveled to Winston-Salem to finish the best-of-three series with a doubleheader, with Durham knotting the series with a first-game victory, followed by Kinston advancing to the championship round with a 6-4 win in the nightcap.

The entire championship series was played in Wilmington because of the hurricane damage, and the Blue Rocks prevailed, three games to one. In their four years of existence, Wilmington had advanced to the finals each year, winning twice.

Lynchburg outfielder Jose Guillen was voted league MVP, posting a .322 average with 21 HR's and 94 RBI. Kinston's Sean Casey won the league batting title at .331, while Freddie Garcia tied teammate Guillen for the home run crown. Johnny Isom of Frederick was the RBI leader with 104 and Wilmington's Sergio Nunez led the league with 44 stolen bases.

Kinston southpaw Noe Najera was named pitcher of the year with a 12-2 record and 2.73 ERA. His manager, Jack Mull, was voted top skipper. Our catcher, Blake Barthol, was named to the year-end All-Star team after hitting .285 with 13 HRs and 66 RBI.

It had been the year of the home run in the majors with 4,962 hit, the most in 128 years of professional baseball. Seventeen players hit 40 or more, smashing the previous record of eight in 1961. The Orioles established a new major league team record with 257. They were led by Brady Anderson's 50, including 12 to lead off games, topping Bobby Bonds record of 11 set in 1973.

The game received another black eye over a spitting incident involving the Orioles Roberto Alomar and umpire John Hirschbeck on the final weekend of the season. Only a court order prevented the umpires from boycotting the post season after Alomar appealed his five-game suspension and was allowed to finish out the season and play-offs.

Much attention was given to the plight of the Atlanta Braves as they were forced to vacate Fulton County Stadium for the Olympics. The Braves played 17 games on the road in 18 days, starting on July 18th. That same day, we concluded an 18-day journey that included 16 consecutive road games.

Unlike the five cities that the Braves traveled to by chartered jet, our players spent over 30 hours on a hot, crowded bus while visiting the same number of cities. Braves players received just under $1,100 each for meal money, while our players were given exactly $217.50 to cover their food.

Despite the Braves' hardship, they fought their way into the World Series again after falling behind St. Louis in the National League Championship Series. The Yankees defeated Texas, then division rival Baltimore, to earn their first trip to the big dance since 1981.

The Braves embarrassed the Yankees in game one, then shut them out in game two to lead 2-0 heading back to Atlanta. But New York came back to win all three in Atlanta before returning home to cap their comeback season with a victory in game six, giving Manager Joe Torre his first world championship.

Our front office situation continued to deteriorate. Morale was at an all-time low as the season was winding down. Dennis Robarge was actively pursuing a job with the National Hot Rod

Association after being passed over when Oster was brought in to become General Manager.

Nearly everyone close to the situation felt that if it were indeed necessary to pass my General Manager duties on to someone else, Dennis should have been the choice. Even Jack Bogaczyk had written a column in the *Roanoke Times* at the end of the season stating as much, and also proclaiming the club had blown a golden opportunity by doing a terrible job of selling season tickets. He pointed out that raising ticket prices and dropping ticket books was part of the reason for the lack of success.

Kelvin was furious after reading the article and accused me of putting Bogaczyk up to writing it. He said I was undermining him and he would not tolerate it. He refused to believe that I had nothing to do with it, and also claimed that I had given Bogaczyk our season ticket totals. I reminded Kelvin that Bogaczyk had written a column in late June, quoting Dave Oster on our season ticket numbers. Kelvin refused to listen to me, even though the June 26th column clearly indicated where the season ticket information came from.

From that point on Kelvin barely spoke to me. Shortly thereafter he revised the employee job descriptions, taking away more of my duties and turning them over to Oster. My end-of-season bonus was significantly lower than in recent years, and he justified it by saying we hadn't done as well as expected at the gate.

Whose fault was that? I had done everything that I was assigned to do and more. I sold nearly fifty percent of our advertising and was the only staff member to exceed my pre-season sales goal. I fulfilled all of my office duties in an efficient and timely manner. What more could I do? Apparently, loyalty, hard work, and dedication meant nothing. I'd become expendable.

*A Youth League Clinic at Salem Memorial
Baseball Stadium, June, 1996.*

Kelvin and I met on October 23rd and again on October 28th, and at that time I submitted a letter of resignation, effective October 31st, 1996. The resignation was made public on November 7th, and I immediately received about a dozen job offers. Included was a group of investors interested in buying a professional baseball team, but only if I would agree to take part ownership and operate it for them.

Dennis submitted his resignation shortly after mine, accepting a General Manager's position with the NHRA at a track just outside of Atlanta.

Two days before Thanksgiving, on November 26th, the major league owners ratified an agreement with the major league players' association by a vote of 26-4. It was the same agreement they had rejected just three weeks earlier by an 18-

12 margin. The approval came exactly one week after White Sox owner Jerry Reinsdorf signed free agent Albert Belle to a record $55 million, five-year contract, shattering baseball's salary structure. Reinsdorf had been one of the more outspoken opponents of the new agreement.

The contract was for a period of five years, retroactive to include the '96 season, with an option year in 2001 at the players' discretion. It provided for interleague play, as well as revenue sharing for small market teams. In addition, the minimum major league salary would be increased to $150,000 and the major leagues would be allowed to expand by two more teams providing the teams are determined by December 31st, 1999 and begin play by 2002.

# 17 An Overview

The game has changed tremendously from a business standpoint in the short time I've been involved. For many years, minor league clubs were community-owned or run as "mom and pop" type operations, with little concern for profits and somewhat lacking in professionalism. When clubs changed hands, it was often for the debt owed by the club or very little money. The successful teams were barely turning a profit, and many clubs just tried to keep their losses to a minimum.

In recent years, all that has changed considerably. Due to supply and demand, minor league clubs are being sold for exorbitant amounts of money. Many people who would like to own their own pro baseball team may not have the resources to own a major league club. They have discovered the minor leagues to be the next best thing, and in some ways even better, considering that in the minors you don't have to deal with player salary issues. But because there is a limited amount of opportunity to own even a minor league team, existing clubs have commanded top dollar when being sold, and these prices have brought a new breed of owner into the minors, following a trend started in the majors leagues.

Whether or not this is good for the game is a matter of opinion. On the negative side, many of these new owners are not "baseball people", meaning they have no baseball background, which can lead to problems in understanding the intricacies of what is needed to perpetuate the game. I believe this has a lot to do with some of the current problems that exist in major league baseball.

The high prices being offered for current franchises have also led some very good baseball people to sell their ballclubs, essentially taking the money and running. Others have chosen to get out of the game because of increased regulations being placed on them by major league baseball. Losing these people is not a positive development as the game enters a new era with many problems that need to be solved.

By the same token, with prices as inflated as many feel they are, not many people from the minor league ranks can afford to buy into a club. Also because of the high prices being paid, many new owners are looking for a quick return on their investment and are willing to move a club, if necessary, to get into a new, efficient stadium in a large market where the potential to turn a big profit is greater.

On the positive side, many of the new owners bring with them strong business backgrounds, good business sense, and, in many cases, greater financial resources. Thus they are able to run a much more professional, businesslike operation with a strong emphasis on marketing.

Additionally, the game itself has progressed immensely in terms of marketing, with a national licensing program through Major League Baseball Properties having developed as an offshoot of the PBA prior to the 1991 season. The biggest benefits of this program are quality-control regulations placed on all companies producing products bearing club logos, and the establishment of relationships with many manufacturers leading to the exposure of minor league logos on merchandise all over the country: this visibility adds credibility to the clubs in the eyes of the public, when they see merchandise sporting minor league logos displayed side by side with that of major league baseball, the NFL, NHL, and NBA.

An additional benefit of the licensing arrangement is the payment of royalties to all clubs for the rights to reproduce their logos and sell team merchandise. The financial rewards have not been significant yet, but they have shown steady growth nearly every year.

The game has also changed from a player relations standpoint since the new PBA went into effect. Some of the changes may simply be a reflection of our society in general, but there appears to be a much greater feeling of separation between the players and the minor league front offices.

In the standard player contract, the players are obligated to help promote the club in their communities via appearances and the use of their likenesses for promotional purposes. It has always been somewhat difficult to get players to sacrifice their personal time for promotional appearances, but in the past few years, it has become nearly impossible. The majority of today's players are not willing to do anything without being paid. We have no problem with paying a player if the club is making money off that appearance, but in many cases, these appearances are made to schools and youth recreational clubs, as a service to help build community relations, with no fee being charged by the club.

Minor league baseball today is definitely a business. Many people want to work in pro baseball because they love the game and feel they can rub elbows with the players and sit around watching games. It certainly helps to love the game if you plan to work in it, but sitting around and watching games is very rare in the operations I've been around. You are usually too busy with your game responsibilities to enjoy this luxury. Many operators will travel when time permits to see their team play on the road so they can actually enjoy the game and learn something about their players. A job in pro baseball requires plenty of hard work, long hours, and, for the most part, especially in entry level positions, very low pay. In addition, there is little stability. It is not uncommon for baseball executives to spend years jumping all over the country striving for a good job, stable organization, and job security.

Clubs also tend to change hands, and often, for no reason at all, you can lose your job simply by being in the wrong place at the wrong time. Not a pleasant thought for someone who has worked his heart out for a club, but such is the nature of this business of baseball.

One of the most popular questions received is "How many of the players will make it to the major leagues?" This is tough to answer because you can never predict from season to season which players have the necessary skills and are going to work hard enough to advance to that level.

One of the more recent, and more accurate, studies was conducted several years ago by *Baseball America* editor Allen Simpson. He looked at all players signed to pro contracts between 1982-1984, to allow adequate time to determine their fate. Of 3,809 players analyzed, 405, or 10.6 percent, made it to the majors. Many play there for only a brief time, but nonetheless, do make it to "The Show".

The chances also increase with each level attained, showing a nine percent success rate at short season A, as compared to 73 percent at Triple-A. At the full-season Class A level, the success rate is 15 percent.

Another question often asked is, "How important is a winning ballclub?" It's been a while since I've known this luxury but, surprisingly, we saw only about a ten to twenty percent increase in fan attendance during those seasons. Because the play of the team is something that the minor league front office has no control over, most clubs rely primarily on promotions or special events to put people in the seats.

This side of the game deals primarily with the business of entertainment. That's the way it should be approached. The goal is to provide good, clean, wholesome, family entertainment at affordable prices. There is a hardcore nucleus of baseball fans who attend games regularly, but the key to success is to draw the casual fan to supplement this nucleus. These are the people looking for something to do on any given night. That's where the special events come into play. Concerts, souvenir giveaways, special celebrity appearances, and even contests and lucky number prize giveaways are the things that make it more than a ballgame!

My first Baseball Winter Meetings in Nashville, Tennessee in 1983 were overwhelming. Attending seminars and listening to people talk about how to market the game successfully, how to operate concessions more efficiently, and how to display souvenirs to maximize sales, seemed too good to be true.

We were learning from the best in the business. Larry Schmittou of the Nashville Sounds, Bill Valentine of the Arkansas Travelers, Art Clarkson of the Birmingham Barons, and Jim Paul of the El Paso Diablos were just a few of the many operators who greatly influenced my approach to this fine game.

Jim Paul has probably done more to perpetuate the game than anyone in recent years through seminars he conducts annually in El Paso. Steve DeSalvo of the Greenville Braves also was instrumental in putting together sales seminars for baseball people for several years. Business seminars are also conducted at the Winter Meetings each year. These opportunities to share ideas and learn from the best are invaluable.

One of the major positives of working in minor league baseball, especially the lower minors, is that you have a much greater opportunity to be involved in the entire operation. It is much more "hands on" than the majors or even the upper minors, where people tend to be more departmentalized.

In the lower minor leagues, you tend to have your hand on the pulse of the entire operation. There is nothing more satisfying than seeing a special event take shape, from the formulative stages, to selling the concept to a sponsor, following up on all details, then harvesting the fruits of your labor on the night of the event.

Every year clubs receive hundreds of resumes from candidates wanting to work in pro baseball. One of the first questions I've always asked a job applicant is, "Why do you want to work in baseball?" If the answer is because they love watching ballgames, I tell them to save themselves a whole lot of aggravation and disappointment and buy a season ticket instead! Each year many clubs hire interns. It's a win-win situation, providing the club with some inexpensive labor, while allowing the intern to pick up valuable experience that could lead to a full-time position.

Many of the people that I've worked with over the years are no longer involved in the game. Bobby Bragan Jr. sold the Elmira club after the 1986 season to a group headed by Clyde Smoll for a reported $265,000. Bobby and his family then moved to Las Vegas, and at last report were still living there. Talk about letting a kid loose in a candy store!

Marty Nash, my assistant in Elmira, stayed in Burlington, North Carolina as the General Manager from 1986-88. After the '88 season, he became the Durham Bulls director of sales and marketing. He left the Bulls late in the '91 season to take a job with the Carolina Thunderbirds of the East Coast Hockey League. The Thunderbirds were in the process of moving to Wheeling, West Virginia, where Marty now serves as assistant General Manager and director of marketing.

Thom Shannon, the former Elmira General Manager under investigation for the disappearance of player rent money in 1982-1983, was never formally charged. He returned to baseball as the General Manager of the Erie club in the New York-Penn League in 1985, then moved over to the Newark team in the same league in '86 and '87. In 1988 he became General Manager of the Rockford Expos in the Midwest League, but in December of that year was charged by the club with felony theft, when it was determined that over $100,000 in team checks had been deposited by Shannon into his own personal checking account. Shannon later pleaded guilty to a reduced charge of deceptive practices, a Class 4 felony, was sentenced to a two-year probation. He agreed to pay back $107,550.53 to resolve the charges. Shannon said in a deposition that he took the money to gamble it into a fortune so he could buy his own team and repay the Expos.

Mike Bucci has also left the game. After managing at Salem in '86, he went to work for the Cleveland Indians organization as a coach at Triple-A Buffalo in '87. In '88, he returned to managing, with the Burlington Indians of the Appalachian League. Incidently, Marty Nash was the General Manager of that club. Bucci resigned prior to the '89 season, and at last report was living in the Philadelphia area where he stays in touch with the game by running a batting cage and conducting area baseball camps for the Phillies each year.

No one knows for certain where the game is headed. There are many problems that need to be dealt with, especially on the major league level. Unfortunately, these problems will ultimately trickle down from our big league counterparts.

Major league baseball must look at ways to cut costs and increase revenues if it is to prosper. The most logical answer is to cut back on the outlandish salaries being paid to today's players. That sounds simple enough, but the only time it was effectively implemented the owners were taken to court by the players union, found guilty of collusion, and forced to pay a huge settlement to a number of players.

There has been talk in recent years of doing away with the farm system as it currently exists. But unlike in football and basketball, it has generally been felt that major league baseball requires a much greater refinement of the levels of skill than can be developed in most college programs. The fact that so few players actually come right out of the college ranks to play immediately in the big leagues is evidence that this is true.

Although the player development budgets for most major league teams are a drop in the bucket compared to the big league payrolls, it's not totally out of the question that the major leagues will try to cut some costs by revamping the current minor league structure. It would be possible to trim some of the excess, streamlining the number of minor league affiliates each club supplies players to. This would not be as dramatic an approach as doing away with the present system altogether, but it would force the major league clubs to give up on fringe players and concentrate on the top prospects. Many fringe players have gone on to become major league superstars over the years, but the money saved could outweigh the occasional prospect that slips through the cracks.

One of the strongest arguments against cutting back on player development is the fact that two of the teams that currently spend the most money in this area, the Toronto Blue Jays and the Atlanta Braves, are two of the most successful franchises in the major leagues.

Another strong possibility is that major league baseball will look to the minor league operators to pick up greater shares of the farm team expenses each time the Professional Baseball Agreement is reopened. Unfortunately, not all minor league clubs are profitable enough to absorb another hit like the last one, and many of the less profitable teams could be forced out of business, sold, or moved into more profitable cities and/or stadiums.

Pro baseball has endured numerous hardships, both real and perceived, during more than 125 years of existence. This is not the first time the game has faced predictions of gloom and doom. Everything is relative and, in many ways, these problems are no worse than many other obstacles that have been overcome in the long history of the game.

TV ratings have been showing a downward trend, and the golden goose of television revenue is no longer as lucrative as it once was. It remains ever important that the game stick to the Bill Veeck philosophy of always treating the customer right, as it is ultimately this customer, the fan, who foots the bill in the form of ticket, concession, and souvenir purchases, as well as radio and television ratings points.

The game is making progress in some key areas. Strict new anti-violence and anti-tobacco rules have been successfully implemented in the minors, but both remain a problem in the majors, where the strength of the players' union makes it very difficult to enforce disciplinary action.

Putting things somewhat in perspective was Rocky Bridges, when asked if he would adhere to the rule banning tobacco use by minor league players and coaches. "I'll give up tobacco when the major leagues do something about the use of cocaine by players like Steve Howe and Darryl Strawberry!" he responded.

I don't know all the answers, but I do know this much: If the game is to survive and continue to prosper, it will take a joint effort by everyone involved. Much of the petty bickering and foolish jousting must be cast aside so that everyone can work together for the benefit of the game, to come up with workable solutions to solve problems in a manner that everyone can live with.

The new agreement between the players and owners is a step in the right direction. Profit sharing for small-market teams could help ease some of the financial burden they experience in trying to compete with the clubs with unlimited resources. Interleague play, especially rivalies such as the Yankees-Mets, Dodgers-Angels, and Cubs-White Sox has also helped attendance and broadcast ratings.

Guaranteeing at least four years of peace could be the most important development to come out of the agreement, as most agree that the strike that wiped out the '94 World Series and the start of the '95 season was more damaging than anyone could have anticipated.

Abraham Lincoln said, "A house divided against itself cannot stand!" That statement holds true today in the game of baseball. Both the leadership and players have to put the good of the game above individual and personal gains. Only when this happens, will this great game again start moving forward. They have taken a step in that direction. For the sake of the game, let's hope they continue.

# 18 Sports Marketing Guidelines

### I

**A. Be Positive! Positive! Positive!** Always speak in a positive manner about your team, league, players, etc. Work at getting every staff member to buy into the "Positive" program as well. Even though things are not always perfect, not always the way you would like them to be, when given lemons, make lemonade! Always try to find something positive within and turn a negative into a positive. You'll be amazed at how quickly the perception of your product improves.

Remember: Perception becomes reality. If you believe in yourself and your product, and you can successfully (and enthusiastically) convey this belief to others, they will believe also.

**B. Develop a regular schedule** of issuing news releases.

Get to know all of your local and regional media people. Keep in mind that they can be your greatest asset. They can get your word out to thousands of people instantaneously. The word-of-mouth promoting your product done by you and your staff on a daily basis is great, but the media can augment it tremendously. Maintaining a regular schedule of issuing news releases, especially during the off-season, will do wonders toward keeping your club name prominent in your community.

**C. Get into the schools.** Career days, reading-incentive programs, and discounted ticket programs geared toward the youngsters in your community provide tremendous opportunities to expand your fan base. Today's children are tomorrow's season ticket holders and event sponsors. They are also loyal fans and will bring parents and friends with them to your events.

**D. Line up public appearances** and speaking engagements for your players and front office staff, to expand your fan base. Every time someone from your organization speaks to a group, you have an opportunity to educate and entice them to sample your product. It is good to have a general outline or promotional videotape as part of the presentation to be sure the major points are covered, as well as to maintain consistency in the presentation regardless of who makes it.

## II

**A. Develop a database.** Find out who your fans are. When people request information on tickets, schedules, souvenirs, etc., get names and addresses. When people come to your arena or ballpark, get them to fill out questionnaires so you can find out who these people are. Offer incentives to get people to fill out questionnaires (such as a pair of free tickets). Also be sure to get names and addresses of all contest entrants and winners. They will come in handy for season ticket and souvenir solicitations via direct mail and/or telemarketing. You can also use questionnaires to find out what your customers think about your operation, including ways to improve your product as well as what they like about it.

**B. Use the phone book.** Telemarketing provides you with another opportunity to expand your database. Using the phone book to sell season tickets or group outings can be a slow, tedious chore, but in the long run will pay tremendous dividends if handled properly. Keep in mind that the person making the calls on behalf of your organization will often be the first (and sometimes only) representative to speak with the person called. Remember the expression "You only have one opportunity to make a first impression" and make sure that your caller realizes that even when a sale is not made, the opportunity to educate the person on the other end of the line exists. You can create a curiosity and an awareness that previously didn't exist. If telemarketing is approached in this positive way, even without making a sale on every call, by educating and creating an awareness of who you are and what you have to offer, you are still making progress every time you pick up the phone.

## III
## Advertise

Advertising is a critical part of every operation. Getting the most bang for your buck is very important. As unique as sports franchises are, it is often quite easy to trade out a large portion of your advertising in exchange for tying local media into specific promotions or events. The greater the media involvement in your program, the more you will benefit. Newspaper, radio, and television are vital ways to get your word out. In addition, the Internet enables you to reach even larger numbers of people on a national basis. It is imperative to know your market. Analyze the people you're trying to reach (and it may be different for different types of events) and determine what method will be the most cost-effective to reach the people in that particular demographic.

In newspaper advertising you rarely need to utilize the sports section because most avid sports enthusiasts read the sports pages and know who you are and when you're playing. Instead, place most newspaper ads in the entertainment section where you can reach the more casual fan or the person looking for something to do.

In many markets, television and radio audiences are heavily fragmented. It pays to be very demographically specific when buying radio or television advertising. Cable television advertising inserts can be extremely cost-effective. For a nominal investment you can often purchase commercial inserts on ESPN, CNN, USA, The Nashville Network, and other stations.

Giving tickets away over the air is one of the most effective radio tools you can use. Many stations look for worthwhile items to give their listeners via contests and as audience-building incentives, and will welcome the opportunity to utilize your tickets. The amount of on-air mentions received each time a pair of tickets is given away usually exceeds the cost of the tickets by a considerable margin. If you anticipate empty seats, the tickets also come in handy by putting additional bodies in the stadium or arena, hopefully giving potential new fans a chance to sample your product, as well as increasing your potential concession and souvenir sales.

**Develop an efficient plan.** It pays to know your market, the people you're appealing to, and the budget you have to work with in order to get you through the entire year. You may want to advertise souvenir merchandise or ticket packages around the holidays. You may want to run a season ticket advertising campaign prior to the start of your season. Rather than running a balanced advertising schedule over the course of your entire season, you may want to go heavier early in the season to get people into the habit of attending your games, with the expectation that the earlier you get them to attend, the more opportunities they will have to return. You can also anticipate their picking up a schedule and telling their friends.

## IV
## Create Media Events

Take advantage of every opportunity to involve the media in your operation. Signing a new player or coach, or landing a major promotional event, deserves at least a news release, but often can include a news conference or media gathering. Don't overuse this tool to the point that you diminish the effectiveness of your major events (remember the boy who cried wolf?) but, by the same token, take advantage of this opportunity whenever you have an event significant enough to draw a media crowd. You can also create events specifically designed for the media such as media/player contests or games, or events pitting different members of the media against one another at your venue. Many events of this type will generate tremendous pre-and-post-event publicity.

## V
## Keep Your Lines of Communication Open

**A. Share ideas.** Talk to other marketing people and operators. Find out what they are having success with. Some of the best marketing people are those who can look at what others are doing and figure out a way to implement those ideas within their framework. Not everything that works for someone else will work for you but, generally, successful ideas can be transformed to fit in other applications if you know your market and are willing to do your homework.

**B. Stay on top of current trends.** New ideas and innovations are constantly evolving. Standards are constantly changing and becoming higher. Competition is also constantly improving, making it tougher to keep up or stay ahead. The need for constant change exists.

**C. Don't be afraid to try something new or different.** If an idea makes sense, try it. Just because no one else has done it before doesn't mean it won't work. Good marketing people are always looking for new ideas. Ideas sell!! It's much easier to get someone excited about what you're trying to accomplish if you have a definite idea and can enthusiastically convey it. Even recycling an old idea is better than no idea at all.

## VI
## Market Your Events

**A. Every event is special.** During your special event (and keep in mind that every game should be treated as a special event), it is imperative to create a carnival-type atmosphere. People are there to have fun. It is your job as an operator to see that they do. You are in the entertainment business. To be successful, people must be entertained. The game, unfortunately, is not always entertaining. You have little control over the game, but you have a great deal of control over the atmosphere you've created surrounding your event.

**B. Everybody is part of the show.** Everyone involved in your game-day activities plays a critical role in your program. Keep in mind the Disney philosophy that everyone is part of the show. It starts with your parking lot attendant and continues with your ticket sellers, ticket takers, ushers, security force, and concession personnel. A bad experience in the parking lot or at the ticket window can be damaging. One of the most difficult parts of your job, but one of the most important, is to get all game-day employees to buy into your program. They are the people in the trenches. They are the people meeting and greeting your public on a daily basis. They can make your fans feel really special when they do their jobs properly.

**C. Your sound system is important.** The music played during your event is also very important. Keep in mind what you are trying to accomplish, and whom you are trying to reach. Try to appeal to the masses. We sometimes get caught up in thinking that everyone likes the same things we like. With most events, you are reaching a broad segment of the population, who have varied interests. Your public address announcer is also one of the most important components of game-day procedures. A good one is vital to a smooth, professional operation.

**D. Provide contests.** People love contests. People love to win prizes. People love trying to win prizes. The more opportunities you give them to do so, the happier they seem to be. Lucky number prizes create excitement. They also help sell programs. Contest entry blanks in your programs also spur sales. The more prize giveaways and contests, the better (within reason, of course). Contests to create audience participation also create audience awareness. In the successful operation, you find people talking as much about the incidental activities as about the game itself.

**E. Do as many things as possible for your fans.** They are the most important part of your operation. Show them your appreciation. Picnics, parties, and other events geared toward your season ticket holders and sponsors are tremendous ways to solidify your relationship with these people. If they are happy and feel good about being involved, they will continue to be so. Booster clubs can play a big part in this area, but it is important to maintain the distinction between the team and the booster club.

## VII
## Always Look at the Big Picture

**Pay attention to detail.** Try to look at your operation from the outside, as a fan would see it. Do you like what you see? If not, you'd better make changes. Even if pleased, strive to keep moving forward, to make it even better. There is always room and need for improvement. To be successful in sports marketing or anything else requires the right attitude and much hard work. If you take care of all the little things, the big things will fall into place.

# Index